The immortality of animals, and
the relation of man as guardian,
from a biblical and philosophical
hypothesis – Primary Source Edition

E D. 1843-1907 Buckner

The Immortality of Animals

And the Relation of Man
as Guardian, from a Biblical
and Philosophical Hypothesis

By

E. D. BUCKNER, A.M., M.D., Ph.D.

PHILADELPHIA

GEORGE W. JACOBS & CO.

PUBLISHERS

O Lord, in whose hand is the soul of every living thing. . .
Thou preservest man and beast —THE BIBLE

————

I would not enter on my list of friends,
Though graced with polished manners and fine sense,
Yet wanting sensibility, the man
Who needlessly sets foot upon a worm —COWPER.

Dedication

To the Society for the Prevention of Cruelty to Animals, Humane Society, Humane Association, Humane Education Society, Anti-Vivisection Society, Anti-Vivisection League, Humanitarian League, Animal Protective League, Humane Alliance, Kindness to Animals Society, Vegetarian Society, Anti-Cruelty Society, Defenders' League, Audubon Society, Band of Mercy, and all other Humane Organizations, the object of which is to Promote Kindness and Prevent Cruelty, this book is prayerfully and hopefully dedicated by

THE AUTHOR.

Preface

THE writing of this book is a duty which was deeply impressed upon my mind many years ago, and which has been more deeply impressed since by reason of the moans and cries of suffering animal life by which I have been surrounded.

I have no ambition to gratify in offering the book to the world beyond the good it may accomplish, in promoting kindness and preventing cruelty.

I have made many statements which I do not pause to explain, but which are based upon positive scientific and historical facts. I have the authorities in my possession for reference when required.

The plan is to show that God, creating the entire universe, the heavens, the earth and all things therein, governs and controls this great cosmos in accordance with an universal law of harmony and goodness.

God has a design in creating one planet as well

as another, and one animal as well as another, and His care extends alike to all.

It is hoped that the object of this book may not be misunderstood and that the spirit of reverence which pervades its pages may not be overlooked. I accept the Bible as a Divine Revelation, and take the Mosaic description of creation as a basis of my work.

It is true that I continue where most theologians leave off. Instead of limiting God's power and goodness, I extend it. Yet I do not claim to have discovered anything new, but only to expand the thought of modern phenomena. What is now known in science is the product of all ages. We of to-day add our little mite to what is handed down to us.

Rome borrowed from Greece, Greece from Egypt, and Egypt, like China, is lost in the mists of historic antiquity, and is supposed to have obtained the light of knowledge from some still earlier civilizations.

The twentieth century is the product of the nineteenth and the nineteenth of the eighteenth. No scientist can grasp all the phenomena of a subject at once; the human faculties are not equal to such an undertaking. Each investigator takes the facts and experiences of others, and then begins to build and expand until he too reaches his limit.

There are theologians to-day who halt and question God's goodness, and His willingness to watch over all His creatures with a tender care, ignoring the fact that God has promised to restore all animal life to primeval peace and happiness.

In consequence they sink into a kind of fatalism, which paralyzes their faculties until they hold no definite ideas regarding the vastness and goodness of God.

From day to day and year to year we are coming in contact with established theories which need reforming and as a consequence modern theology must bend in that direction. Men of education are sometimes ready to object to or repudiate doctrines which lead to an extension of the higher attributes of the Creator, if they seem to oppose long established creeds and dogmas. They naturally wish to find objections to any theory which is out of the usual line of thought, and so take the well-recognized means which have been so often employed in keeping back advancing truths.

The great majority of people drift along, many

times unconsciously, with old exploded ideas, having no desire to fall in with the procession of reformers

There is incredulity from ignorance as well as from knowledge. If the distinguished philosophers during the days of Copernicus had known the facts which were afterwards fully established by him in his philosophy of the solar system, they would not have laughed him to scorn and stigmatized him as a heretic.

The great philosopher Galileo was persecuted and imprisoned and the great philosopher Bruno was burned at the stake for advocating what to-day are accepted astronomical facts, viz.: that the fixed stars are suns scattered through space, accompanied by satellites which bear the same relation to the stars that our earth does to our sun, or our moon to our earth. From the time of Pythagoras down to the present day, a host of men of the highest intellectual powers, as the result of scientific observation and research, have advocated a plurality of worlds. By the use of powerful telescopes and spectroscopes, astronomers are able to see into the blue expanse of the heavens and investigate many satellites which may be inhabitable worlds like ours, provided by the goodness of our Heavenly Father for the future abode of all animal life. This may seem visionary, but I believe, as the years roll on, that God will inspire men with wisdom to discover and to teach some such humane purpose. Many wonderful revelations have come upon the scientists of our time—revelations which the philosophers of the days of Kepler and Newton never thought of; great truths which have confirmed the authenticity of God's revelation to man and man's relation and duties to all creation.

With the great bulk of society, life is merely the following of a few instincts with a perfect blindness as to consequences. By individuals and by communities alike, physical and moral evils are patiently endured, which a true knowledge of the system of Providence would cause to be instantly redressed.

The philosophy set forth in this book extends the principles of humanity to all animal life, and shows the near relation of man to other animals in physical and mental phenomena. The doctrine is advocated that we are morally bound to respect the feelings and rights of animals as descendants from the same Creator, even as we do those of our human associates.

From obeying these moral laws, we shall reap as certain a harvest of benefits to ourselves as by obeying any other code of laws ever established The various forms of wanton cruelty which have hitherto prevailed throughout the world's history will cease when the day of knowledge herein advocated is ushered in through the glorious light of the true revelation of God's purposes.

Viewing Him as the Creator of all living things, and seeing that the whole of creation is constructed upon a plan of benevolence and justice, we expand to loftier, more generous and more holy emotions as we feel that we are only a part of a system, much of which has not yet been revealed.

The place man holds as compared with the whole universe of God's creation is humble beyond all statement of degrees. Man, considered zoologically and without regard to the distinct characters assigned to him by theology, simply takes his place as an animal of the mammalia class, and nothing more.

Above him is the higher creation of angels, archangels, cherubim and seraphim, and of innumerable worlds of which we know very little.

The theory of the immortality of animals is

advocated throughout this book from a Biblical and philosophical hypothesis. There is a law in physics that nothing is lost, and so we reason. All potential forces and substances in nature are indestructible and eternal. Matter and soul—or mind—are the only constituent elements in the universe, and they both exist alike in man and in the lower animals. The body, which is matter, changes its form at death; but that mysterious life potency, known as the soul or mind, is immaterial and immortal, and returns to God who gave it.

Man and the lower animals are not immortal from choice, but because the Creator has decreed it, and what God has created He alone can annihilate. That there will be a general restoration of all animal life is the most liberal and reasonable conclusion of modern theology. That God has made ample provision and revealed sufficient evidence for such restoration is offered in good faith. But this is not offered as an incentive for man to be kind to animals, as it makes no difference whether they have souls or not, the obligation remains the same. We do not stop to ask whether a helpless woman or child has a soul when we see one in distress or cruelly treated, neither should we ask the question about any other suffering being. There are kind-hearted people who do not believe the Bible, and consequently do not believe that either man or lower animals have souls; yet they recognize the moral law of kindness to all living creatures as much as some Christians, and, many times, even more.

If the Church was more active and liberal in extending the knowledge of God's attributes of goodness and mercy over all His creatures, she might have more friends and adherents

The spirit of charity has been so carefully observed throughout this volume that I believe there is not a sentence or word used which will tend to lower or reflect upon the dignity of any animal or its mode of life.

No mention is made of animals preying one upon another, as I regard this state of depravity in the same light as the preying of men upon each other; namely, the result of the original sin of man, which caused the fall of all living beings from primeval peace and happiness. In order to make this work of a permanent nature, I have avoided the use of such events as I thought might become trite and out of date.

The arguments on the leading subjects could be greatly extended, but the work has been condensed to meet the exactions of a busy world. The whole ground of the animal question has been considered in its various phases, but the main feature of the work is the " Immortality of Animals," and a plea for their kind treatment.

So far as I have been able to ascertain, in this country and in Europe, this is the only work ever published which treats of the immortality of animals from a Biblical and philosophical hypothesis, or from the standpoint of revealed and natural theology. As there is a growing demand for humane literature, it is hoped that this work may be given a wide circulation by the friends of the cause. Finally, I offer this book to the world with the prayer that God in His infinite goodness and mercy may put it into the hearts of mankind to be more kind and merciful to all living creatures.

E D. Buckner.

Introduction

MANY subjects of transcendent importance are
shrouded in inherited misconceptions and vague
prejudices. They await congenial temperaments, in-
dustry, and the peculiar intelligence necessary to present them in their true lights, tempered to compre-
hensions fatigued by the incessant cares of active life.
Some of these appeal to the loftiest conceptions
and emotions; they protrude themselves with such
force as to overwhelm the disposition to lay them
aside for consideration at a more convenient season.
Dr Buckner has chosen one of the most touching
of them, confronting us with duties and responsibilities, of which we have been scarcely conscious,
and has been successful in catching the discordant
tones and arranging them in a pleasing symphony.

He reminds us that nothing is annihilated in
the processes of nature; even in death there is a
mere diffusion or rupture in the relationship of certain chemical elements of which the body is com-

posed, to assume other functions, the decomposition dissolving the ephemeral dwelling of man's spiritual essence, summoned elsewhere, perhaps to bear witness to deeds done in the flesh, perhaps to take rest until the day when it shall be called upon to resume its offices in a rehabilitated body.

The Unity of Life is no longer in controversy; science has reluctantly been driven to accept it, and intelligence finds a ready solution of wearying inconsistencies in the reasonable conviction that all animals have the same origin with man; receive the same parental solicitude in infancy; display the same mental attributes in varying degrees consistent with their calling; possess similar passions, from exquisite tenderness to savage brutality; perform the duties assigned to them with commendable integrity, receiving from man the infamous return of ingratitude and treachery while they partake to the fullest extent in the results of his fall. In short, as all have the same origin and experiences in life, as all die the same death, all shall share the same destiny. If salvation be made perfect through suffering; if felicity shall be granted to man in consideration of a well spent life and in recompense for his mundane sufferings, how can his innocent and trusting companions, constant and true as they have been from infancy to death, fail of some similar eternal reward ?

The most eminent scientist of this country, Agassiz, thoroughly believed in the immortality of animals. More than one hundred and seventy English authors, lay and clerical, uphold it and have written in its support, and the belief is gaining ground steadily. Whoever desires light upon the subject and approaches the perusal of Dr. Buckner's book with a sympathy for all God's creatures, will not fail to obtain the solace which his spirit needs, and a much enlarged sense of man's responsibilities towards his humbler fellow-creatures, with an additional interest in them and in their welfare.

Dr. Buckner claims with justice that animals were given us as companions to contribute to our gratification and reasonable service, and moreover shows that God breathed into their nostrils the breath of life as He did into ours; and that the Scripture conveys and reiterates the assurance that they possess, with mankind, souls, and shall be delivered from the bondage of corruption into an abode of future happiness.

The author discourses fluently upon these subjects and with authority, clinging with conscientious scruple to what is upright and comely, and he illustrates his points with precision and delicacy. He has been careful to avoid cause of offense, and nowhere are his claims unreasonable.

He treads the fields of philosophy as well as the sacred and fragrant gardens of revelation, and his methods of availing of their fertility are profitable and convincing.

The whole question is treated by competent authority, and is replete with intense interest; the book should commend itself to universal attention.

H. O. HAUGHTON,
Editor of *The Dawn.*

Baltimore, Md., March 20, 1903.

Contents

The Immortality of Animals

CHAPTER I

INTERPRETATION OF THE BIBLE —CREATION

Revealed theology—Definition of words—Bible definition of soul
—It belongs alike to man and lower animals—God has decreed
that all creatures that possess the breath of life shall live forever.

WHETHER death terminates the existence of animal life or gives to that existence a new and more
vigorous impulse in another world, is a question
which has undergone various changes in different
epochs of theological history. But sages and philosophers of all ages have taught that man and the
lower animals are animated by some higher principle than mere matter and motion, and that the
principle called soul, or mind, is independent of the
body, and is immaterial and immortal. The word
soul in its original signification stood for the principles which govern life both in man and the lower

animals.   It is true that the modes of explaining it were various   Sometimes it was regarded as the mere harmony of the bodily functions, and some times as a distinct entity of higher ethereal nature, but no essential distinction was made between the soul of man and the soul of the lower animals until a comparatively recent date.

The mental differences between the lower animals and man suggested to ancient philosophers that there should be a line drawn somewhere.   To meet this distinction the Stoics, the disciples of Socrates, maintained that man possessed a rational soul above that of the animal soul which belonged in common to man and animals, but nowhere denied the fact of animals having souls.   This gracious privilege of denying the right of animals to keep the soul their Creator gave them comes from our modern theology, and is ingrafted in the creeds of some of our churches.   But whatever distinction has been made between the soul of man and the soul of animals has been made by man and not God.

In considering this metaphysical and psychological subject I shall attempt to deal with it as a single phenomenon of nature which is to be interrogated for its evidence, without any solicitude for the fate of a preconceived theory, and without asking how this evidence is to be reconciled with that derived from other sources I claim that no sentiment or fact plainly contained in the Scriptures need be refused or contradicted on account of its apparent incongruity with systematic theology. By this liberal interpretation only is it possible for the whole amount of religious knowledge intended to be imparted by the Scriptures to be gathered from them. It is a deplorable fact that many Christians are so accustomed to a certain creed and dogma of their own that they will adhere to it even at the sacrifice of the great moral laws of love and of mercy. We are too liable to forget that those who differ from us may be just as sincere and honest in their belief and just as competent to form a correct interpretation of the Scriptures as we are. And it must be admitted that after all possible scientific research, we can scarcely penetrate beyond the exterior movement of the material system; while the vast interior mechanism of nature is concealed and is in itself strictly incomprehensible by human knowledge.

It must be granted as certain that whatever

relates to infinity; to the divine nature; to the
ultimate purpose of the divine government; to the
unseen worlds and to the future state, and even to
the mechanism of motives in the great cosmos, must
offer itself to the human understanding in a form
beset with mysteries and difficulties.

If therefore we resolve to receive from the
Inspired Writings nothing but what we can reconcile with certain abstruse notions and partial interpretation of passages, the consequence is inevitable:
we shall obtain a very limited and pitiful system of
theology.

It is reasonable to suppose that there are treas-
ures of divine knowledge yet latent beneath the
surface of the divine writings which the practice of
scholastic exposition so long adhered to, on all sides,
has locked up from the knowledge and use of the
world.

It is to be hoped that when the simple and
humble style of inductive interpretation is better
understood, and more consistently resorted to, and
when the necessary imperfections and incoherency
of all human knowledge of divine things is fully
recognized, we may see a better world.

The vain attempt to fashion a miniature model

of the spiritual universe and limit God's beneficence to a fractional part of His creation must
be abandoned, together with all other narrow,
absurd doctrines, if theology expects to keep up
with modern philosophy.

While the subject of the immortality of animals
is not new, yet I know of no attempt to treat it, as
I have done, from the hypothesis of revealed and
natural theology.

By revealed theology we have been taught to believe in the immortality of the soul. Existence, in
the case of man, has been considered by the Church
from its very foundation, indestructible, and it
is not my purpose to dwell on what is now considered common orthodoxy. The Church teaches that
man and the lower animals have to die, that all souls
are immortal, and that all men have souls. This being admitted I am required only to prove that
lower animals have souls.

The main philosophical hypothesis I present is
that the same analogy of logic which can be
adduced to demonstrate the fact that men have
souls will apply to lower animals. In dealing with
the subject it is well at the beginning to define
the meaning of some words.

The word man, in a theological sense, means all the descendants from Adam including both sexes; and in a zoological sense man is an animal, placed as the highest type of the mammalia. The word animal, in a general sense, means all living beings under the various terms of man, beast, fowl, fish, bird, etc., which are classed under various subdivisions. In order to make the distinction clear, I use the ambiguous term lower animals, when I do not wish to include man.

Animal life is that state of existence in which the vital organs are capable of performing their functions. It is that period during which the body and soul are united.

By the functions of animals is understood the operation of the various organs which constitute vital action, therefore life consists of a constant series of actions from the period of birth to the moment of dissolution.

The constituent and essential parts of man and lower animals consist of two things, known in nature as matter and mind, or body and soul. The body was originally made out of the dust of the earth, and the soul is that vital energy breathed into all animals by the Creator. This mysterious life potency of animals which is a separate thing from the body has been known under various names, yet it is commonly recognized as mind or soul, and as that immaterial, immortal principle which goes to form all animal life

There are many words used, in a theological sense, to express the immaterial part of man. The words "soul," "mind," "spirit," "ghost" and "eternal life," are among those most frequently used, but as they all convey the same idea it is of no consequence which is employed. I prefer to use the word "soul" as it was the word God used at the beginning of creation to distinguish the immortal from the mortal part of the body.

Webster's dictionary which has been the standard authority in theology, as well as in other branches of philosophy, for nearly a century, during which time it has undergone various revisions, corrected by the leading theologians of all churches and creeds, defines the mind as "the entire spiritual nature; *the soul.*" And in defining the soul it calls it the "spiritual, rational, and immortal part of man, the seat of real life or vitality." In defining spirit (Heb. ruach, Gr. pneuma, Lat. spiritus) it says it is "life or living substance considered independently of corporal existence. The intelligent, immaterial, and immortal part of man; *the soul*. A disembodied soul, the soul after it has left the body." It gives the definition of the old Saxon word, ghost, as meaning "the spirit or soul." Therefore it is plain that the word *soul* is the best word which can be used to express the immaterial part of a living being.

All other terms such as mind, will, sensation, reason, volition, instinct, etc., are faculties of the soul and subordinate to it, in the same way as the attributes of God are a part of Him. Now we have matter and soul as the only elements of the universe, and lower animals as well as man are composed of these two substances. The soul has a distinct nature and it is a distinct reality from the body; a substance immaterial and essentially different from matter.

That all animals are dual beings possessing a double organism, the one structure being corporal, visible, and tangible, the other incorporal, invisible, and intangible, is an assumption which cannot be disproved.

Man and the lower animals were made out of the same chemical elements, and were given life from the same Creator. That there are grades of being in both man and animals is obvious, but this does not change the Creator's design which has placed all under one common law.

Mind and matter exist in all alike and though there may be a difference in degree there is no difference in kind. In proportion as the functions or relations are more or less perfect, animals ascend and descend in the scale of existence, but nowhere does God show any favoritism on account of such differences.

By the same analogy and logic which is used to prove by the Bible that men have souls, we can equally prove that lower animals have souls.

In the argument in either case we meet with many obscure and seemingly contradictory passages. To comprehend the meaning of the Bible we must take into consideration the original language from which it is derived and the probable prejudice brought to bear on the translators.

Throughout this work I have carefully examined the best authorities and make no statement which cannot be fully substantiated.

It must not be forgotten that our present English version dates back only to 1611, and it is beyond this date that scholars go to ascertain the original meaning of words The Old Testament was written in the Hebrew language and the New Testament in the Greek, but the Bible has undergone various translations. The Septuagint version or translation of the Old Testament into Greek is of vast importance in showing the original language of the Hebrew at that time. And there is to-day a great difference in the opinions of Hebrew and Greek scholars about the meaning of many words in the translation.

The Hebrew text of the Old Testament is acknowledged by all scholars to be the most accurate. Marginal notes and comments are numerous in all of the old translations, but most of them have disappeared from our present English version. It is well to keep in mind that the Hebrew word for the soul is *nephesh* and the Greek word *psyche.* The two words mean the same thing, and the Greek word *psyche* is the only word in the New Testament which is translated *soul.*

Now let us see wherein the Bible implies as well as expresses the doctrine that animals have souls. God in the beginning of time called into existence the heavens, the earth, and all things living and moving therein.

This entire creation was divided into a series of six periods, or epochs, in each of which a new life potency entered into what at that time existed, and called forth new developments which go on according to His law. In the sixth day or epoch, which was the last period of creation, God finished His work by creating all animal life All animals, including man, were formed out of the earth. There was no distinction.

The same term, made, " bara," was used for both man and lower animals. There was no preference given to man over other animals as is usually claimed by modern theology. When God created the lower animals and mankind He included all in the same benediction and " blessed them " and pronounced them " very good."

And in this connection I wish to call attention to the fact that man and lower animals had provided for them the same kind of food, all of which was vegetable. There was no preying upon each other and no death, but all lived at peace as one great, happy family.

In the next chapter of Genesis, in again bringing

up the subject of creation for the purpose of giving
the history of the fall of man, the divine writer
gives the "generation" or history by repeating the
same method, that man and lower animals were
formed out of the earth.

Here, for the first and only time, the particular
manner of how life was imparted was given in the case
of Adam.   The inspired writer says, "God breathed
into his nostrils the breath of life; and man became
a living soul."   As to what methods were used to
impart life to the other animals and to Eve we are
not informed.   But to say that God used one way
for lower animals, one for man and one for woman,
when all were made of the same chemical constituents, would be contrary to any system of analogy
known to reason.   Any Bible student knows that
there are many things understood which are not
expressed throughout the entire Bible, therefore
whatever is understood by the words, "breathed
into his nostrils the breath of life and man became
a living soul," is implied, though it is not expressed,
in the creation of all other forms of animal life.
No animal could live without the breath of life, and
as the divine writer said nothing about the manner
of its being imparted, it must be assumed that God

breathed into the animals and woman, the breath of life and they became living souls Any other assumption would be illogical.

In describing the creation of woman, nothing is said about the breath of life or a living soul. Now must we infer that she, like the lower animals, is denied a soul because the special manner of imparting life is not mentioned? And yet if you deny that animals have souls, because the mode in which they received them is not mentioned, you will certainly have to exclude women from having souls upon the same hypothesis, which has been done by some crude forms of religion. The Bible plainly infers that whatever process was involved in bestowing the breath of life in the case of Adam was followed with all other created beings. In reference to the flood, the inspired writer in Genesis 7: 21, 22, says: "All flesh died that moved upon the earth, both of fowl, and of cattle, and of beasts, and of every creeping thing, and every man, all *in whose nostrils* was the breath of life"

I have so far used the English version in what I have said as to the soul A few facts from older versions I will now mention in evidence.

It is acknowledged by all the best Greek and

Hebrew scholars to-day that, in every passage of Scripture where the Hebrew word *nephesh* or the Greek word *psyche* is used, it should be translated soul, and when *nephesh chayah* is used it should be translated living soul. This is admitted by the marginal reading found in many old English Bibles. In Genesis 2:7, when the divine writer speaks of Adam, the translation is correct, as it reads in the Hebrew, *nephesh chayah*, which translated into English means a living soul; but there are nine more passages in Genesis where the same Hebrew words are used, but as they refer to lower animals the true meaning has been perverted by the English translation.

We read: "God said, Let the waters bring forth abundantly the moving creature that hath a *living soul*." The Hebrew text reads *nephesh*, soul, and *chayah*, living, and the English version has it "life," but on the margin of many Bibles "living soul."

Again we read, "And God created great whales and every *living soul*." Hebrew, *nephesh chayah*, the English version, "living creature." Again we read, "And God said, Let the earth bring forth the *living soul* after its kind, cattle and creeping things and beasts of the earth." This is the proper read-

ing, but the English version has it "living creature."

I will call your attention to one more passage in
this connection: "To every beast of the earth and
to every fowl of the air and to everything that
creepeth upon the earth wherein there is a *living
soul.*"

The Hebrew text is given in plain words *nephesh
chayah.* The English version gives it "life," but in
many Bibles in the marginal reading it is rendered
"a living soul." I have before me a Bible published
in 1867 by the American Bible Society, which gives
in the margin the words "living soul" in this last,
and two more similar passages. I recently examined a large number of Bibles in a repository and
continued my researches until I found one hundred
giving the words "living soul" in the margin where
the word "life" is used in the text of the English
version.

Rev. Dr. Bush, in his commentary on Genesis,
makes the following plain statement: "The phrase
'living soul' is repeatedly applied to the inferior
order of animals. It would seem to mean the same
when spoken of man that it does when spoken of
beasts, viz., an animated being, a creature possessed

of life and sensation, and capable of performing all the physical functions by which life is distinguished, and we find no *terms* in the Bible to distinguish the intellectual faculties of man from the brute creation."

I will call the reader's attention to two more passages wherein the word soul is translated as it should be. In Numbers 31 : 28, God said, "Levy a tribute unto the Lord, *one soul* of five hundred, both of the persons, and of the beeves and of the asses and of the sheep." In Revelations 16 : 3, we find these words: "Every *living soul* died in the sea."

It would be useless to continue these quotations as the reader can see that, if I am correct, the Bible, without the shadow of a doubt, recognizes that animals have living souls the same as man.

Most of the quotations given are represented as having been spoken by the Creator Himself and He certainly knows whether or not He gave to man and lower animals alike a living soul, which of course means an immortal soul, as there cannot be a living soul without its being immortal.

In determining the meaning of the Bible, we should rest our belief, not on what man would have us believe, but on what God would have us believe. If God, in His revealed word, had intended to convey the idea that man was created immortal and animals were not, He certainly would not have made a plain statement that all were created alike.

Comparative psychology is opening up a wonderful field for scientific research, and we are learning to know God's purposes through nature as well as revelation. All animal life is formed upon one common general law, and shows conclusively that if man is a dual being, composed of matter and mind, or body and soul, so are all other animals. If God created one and imparted to it the breath of life and an immortal soul, He made all others on the same plan; for it is obvious that there is that same visible difference between matter and mind in all living beings.

The vital principle which sets in motion the functions of the organism producing thoughts, feelings, sensation, and motion, differs from that which builds up the physical organization. It is common to all sensitive and perceptive living beings, to both man and lower animals, and though the word soul goes under various names, it was used by the inspired writer to convey the idea of a living principle.

The body does not consist merely of matter, of which it may be composed at any given moment, and which is constantly changing, but of that immortal vital energy which can no more die than the immaterial substance known as gravitation, cohesion, or affinity.

We have no evidence on which to affirm that existence once imparted ever has been, or ever will be, absolutely annihilated It may undergo prodigious changes; its combinations may be dissolved, its elements scattered; it may be released from the obligations of one set of laws, and be subject to another totally different; organization may be destroyed, and its component parts broken into a thousand fragments; life may be extinguished; the body may utterly perish; and yet there is no annihilation of the life potency or soul.

Certainly, to reduce any substance into nothing requires just the same power as to convert nothing into something. The Creator, who called all existence into being, could annihilate it all, or any portion of it, just as easily as He gave it birth. Man and lower animals are not immortal from choice but because that beneficent Being who created them has willed that they shall be so. They cannot cease to be because God resolves to uphold them in an eternal existence.

Socrates admitted the immortality of all animal life, and maintained that "the bodies of men and beasts are warm and living as long as they breathe, and as soon as the breath leaves the body, not only do warmth and motion cease, but the body begins to decay. Life, therefore, is breath, and breath is air, and as air is eternal and inseparable in its very nature, therefore the soul or portion of air which gave animation to the body will not perish at the dissolution of the body." Elihu conveys the same idea when he says: "The Spirit of God hath made me, and the breath of the Almighty hath given me life." Therefore if the breath which inflated Adam's nostrils was a particle of Divine essence which imparted immortality to man, then we must conclude that all other animals have the same kind of immortality, for they received the same kind of breath.

As Solomon says of man and the lower animals, "They have all one breath, so that a man hath no preëminence above a beast."

CHAPTER II

THE GARDEN OF EDEN —THE FALL OF MAN AND THE LOWER ANIMALS

All animals in perfect peace and happiness—Man as guardian—No preying on each other, and no death—All commanded to use vegetable food—Cosmical derangement caused by the fall.

THE next important epoch in Bible history which affects alike man and the lower animals, and which I wish to call attention to, is the fall from the happy and exalted position they occupied in the Garden of Eden.

When God created man and the lower animals, He placed them in a large garden of rich fertile soil with an abundance of fruit, nuts, herbs, grass, plants, flowers, and all kinds of vegetation for use and ornament. This garden was abundantly provided with springs, brooks, and rivers.

In order that every kind of animal might have a happy home, God gave them rich valleys, high mountains, and great forests. The earth, teeming with every variety of useful productions, was the great storehouse of the Almighty, from which all living things were commanded to help themselves. They were all vegetarians, for they were commanded by the Creator to live on nothing else. There was no necessity to destroy one life to support another.

Man and lower animals were commanded to multiply and replenish the earth, and sufficient vegetable food was provided for all Man had no more right to kill and eat an animal than he had to kill and eat his own offspring. He was created a frugivorous animal; and his natural food, by his peculiar structure, appears to have consisted of fruits and vegetables

Man's short weak jaws, his canine teeth being equal in length to the remaining teeth, and his tubercular molars, would allow him neither to feed on grass nor to devour flesh, were these aliments not previously prepared by cooking, which art was not discovered until after the fall of man. But when once possessed of the use of fire, and those arts by which man is aided in seizing animals or killing them at a distance, every living being was rendered subservient to his use as well as abuse. By this change of food man's health was impaired, and his life has been growing shorter from age to age.

Man being formed upright, he has the entire use
of his arms and hands which enables him to have
superiority over other animals in many respects;
and this, together with his cunning and intelligence,
has enabled him to tame, or repulse, or destroy,
other animals and thus become the "king of beasts"
or the "lord of creation." This was the result of
the fall; for before that sad event all lived together
as one great happy family, and Adam was the
guardian of them all. He called them by name;
he had named "every living soul" and he was kind
and affectionate to them as their foster father.
They understood a language by which they were
able to communicate with each other. Adam and
Eve made their clothing out of vegetable products.
There were no deaths before the fall, and consequently no skins were used for clothing until after
that event.

As each statement made by the inspired writer
usually represents a period of many years, sometimes thousands, there is no doubt that man and
the lower animals lived in the Garden of Eden, a
peaceful happy family, for a great number of years
before the fall.

In this primeval innocence, there was surpassing

beauty in every animate and inanimate object, and every living thing in the heavens above and all that moved in the waters or upon the earth below, were at peace.

There was no fear of harm, and one hymn of harmony and order ascended to the Creator from all the tribes of earth and heaven. Well might the angels sing and shout together for joy. A beautiful order prevailed through all the various gradations, from the lowest lifeless matter, up to the fairest flower in the vegetable kingdom and the tallest cedar in the garden of God; and thence on up through all the orders possessed by beautiful, happy, and noble animals, to man, who was to have dominion over all other animals. And to fit him for this guardianship he was given superior intellect and a dignified, upright, physical form. As he was made guardian, the animals were affected by his acts for good or evil, happiness or misery. All things were placed under man even as he was under God. It was his rank to inherit the world, and his business to beautify and honor and extend his dominion.

He was a father to all and they were under his parental care and keeping. He, with all other creatures, was pronounced "very good," and in that respect represented the moral image of God. All animals were created in the image of God in the sense of being innocent, and as having the power of motion, will, understanding, and freedom to act; but in no respect were man and the lower animals created in the *nature* of God. In a physical and moral sense man no more resembles God than the lower animals do; for God is a Spirit, without body or parts, and is both visible and invisible, while man and the lower animals are dual beings of both soul and body.

Man and woman, then without the shadow of guilt, were wandering through the rich garden of the earth as the ornaments of all creation; stopping now and then perhaps to stroke the mane of a lion, or to caress the affectionate dog, or to watch the amusing antics of some playful animal, or to listen to the sweet songs of the birds, or to pluck now and then a beautiful flower. They were in the midst of perfect peace and happiness. No need to worry, for God would take care of them all.

The Biblical narrative suggests a beautiful and happy picture of that first life. The young lions and lambs scampered over the green sod and tumbled

over each other, while their fond mothers watched
the playful antics of their precious little ones. The
eagle and the dove, perched upon the same branch
of the great oak, cooed and called to each other.
The sweet songs of the birds mingled together
as they darted from branch to branch on the trees
along the banks of the river Pison. The cattle
wandered down to the river Hiddekel to quench
their thirst and to lie in the cool shade. The
playful monkeys scampered up and down the trees
on the banks of the river Gihon. The intelligent
dogs mingled with all other animals and had their
share of the joys of life. The noble horse and
the nimble deer galloped over the plains and rich
valleys of Assyria and drank of the pure water
of the Euphrates. All animals were contented
and happy, and mingled their voices in the praise
of their Creator.

Adam and Eve received from the kind hands of
their Creator blessings innumerable and precious,
and no doubt they at first cherished in their
hearts the warmest feelings of gratitude. The
lovely scenes of nature which surrounded them,
exciting their daily admiration, appeared in their
view as a mirror on whose polished surface they

might trace the reflected wisdom and goodness of God.

The murmuring streams and gentle breeze whispered God's name; the birds floating in the air, the cattle grazing in the fields, the sagacity of the elephant and the dog, the human-like cunning of the monkey, the beautiful plumage of the peacock, all bespoke His goodness and wisdom; and the heavens above and the earth beneath all portrayed His power and love. Would that we could stop here, and draw a curtain over the dismal future and hide historical facts. The imagination faints beneath its own conception of the great and awful transformation which follows. This change is the saddest epoch in man's history.

While man was surrounded with the law of nature which was impressed on his mind by the design and beauty of what he observed, God had given him a positive law, under penalty of death in case he should violate it; and as the result man, the most dignified of the whole creation, was the first to derange this grand cosmical system by breaking the law and entailing on himself and on the lower animals death and every form of misery, sin, and sorrow with which we are to-day surrounded.

Then it was, when God's law was violated and dishonored, that darkness usurped the place of light, discord the place of harmony, pollution the place of purity, sorrow the place of joy, and cruelty the place of mercy.

There was not an animal of the field, nor a fowl of the air, nor a fish of the water, nor a flower of the garden, nor a tree of the forest, nor a stream in the valley, nor a breeze in the air, but was involved and affected by man's fall; for all fell with him.

As the result, man was driven from the garden never again to gaze upon it. The very spot was cursed and blotted out from all future recognition; and briars, thorns, thistles, deserts, and desolation were spread over that part of the earth. Everywhere and in everything to-day we see signs and evidences of the curse inflicted upon the world for man's sin   Man, instead of having that sinless, holy image of God, soon plunged into jealousy, falsehood, and murder. His history has ever since been a history of sin, cruelty, carnage, bloody deeds, and wars.

There is not an ache, nor a pain, nor a moan, nor a cry in animal life but is due to the fall of man. What was once innocent, happy, affectionate animal nature was changed to a more savage nature. Thus, as the consequence of man's sin, the lower animals, which were not guilty of sin nor had any lot or part in the cause of the fall, are made to undergo a share of his punishment. This is the sad condition which draws into the same abyss of physical and moral misery the whole creation of which Adam was the head as guardian.

> "See the countless multitude above us,
>   Claiming sympathy—our humble kin,
> Sadly have they learned to fear and doubt us,
>   Driven from our side by human sin,
> Yet, though dumb, their hearts to ours are speaking,
> Help and kindness from us ever seeking.
>   Kindness hard to win.

> "Innocent of wrong, our own transgression
>   Lays on them a heavy load of pain,
> Sharing all the misery and oppression
>   Man has wrought beneath his iron reign.
> Touch all hearts, O Thou Divine Compassion,
>   Till they burn with generous love and passion
>   To remove the stain "

There are many mysteries in connection with the fall of man, but the result is obvious. That the lower animals were immortal before the fall is as clearly taught as that man was immortal.

The Old Testament tells us · how the soul originated and why it is immortal, and the New

Testament confirms what was said in the Old Testament. The Bible does not say, in so many words, that either man or lower animals were immortal before the fall, but certainly infers that both were.

There are many things in the Bible which must be understood, though they may not be expressed, or the text would have no meaning whatever. This is true of the command not to eat of the forbidden fruit. The command was not given to the woman, as is generally taught. Adam received the command before Eve was created, and if she ever received the command it must be implied, because it is not expressed. If man had not violated the law given him, he and all other animals would not only have had the continuance of their souls and bodies but would probably have been transported to an upper paradise or higher heaven in some distant planet where sufficient room had been prepared for all.

CHAPTER III

THE CHRISTIAN ERA —THE RESTORATION FROM THE FALL

The atonement sufficient to include the salvation of lower animals—All on an equality—The original purpose of the Creator cannot be fulfilled until animals are restored to the condition they enjoyed before the fall.

THE Christian era is the next important part of Bible history which affects man and lower animals.

Though man had fallen by his disobedience to the Divine law, God, in His infinite love and mercy, made a provision for his relief. A deliverer was promised who would conquer the enemy, and so that which was lost in the fall should be restored.

Christ, according to Divine purpose, came in the fulness of time to be the Saviour of the lost, and by virtue of His suffering and death, all under certain conditions are justified from the curse of the law.

" As in Adam all die, so in Christ shall all be made alive " According to the accepted doctrine of modern theology, the Bible teaches that man everywhere is required to believe that Christ is the true Messiah, and then to repent of his sins, conform to the rules of the Church, and live a consistent Christian life, in order to be saved.

Modern theology takes the broad view that salvation was commensurate with all conditions, and of intrinsic value sufficient to expiate the sins of the whole world; that "Christ is the propitiation for our sins, not for ours only, but for the sins of the whole world."

Modern theology makes conditions for this salvation; but for those who are deprived of the privilege of hearing the gospel, and for those who may hear but cannot understand, the atonement has been made sufficient.

The greatest number of God's creatures come under the latter clause, which includes the heathen, idiots, children, and animals. Animals cannot understand the plan of salvation, and are not under the moral law, for "where no law is there is no transgression."

The New Testament teaches that suffering innocence, under all conditions, shall be rewarded in the final administration of justice, and as animals are not subject to any moral law and cannot sin, there must be a future reward for their untold suffering in this life.

A man who is capable of understanding the moral law which has been given him may violate it and forfeit every advantage he was capable of possessing, and have nothing left him but the sad expectation of a dreadful sentence and a terrible doom.

In such a deplorable situation we often hear men wish they were animals, or at least as innocent as a dove or a lamb. And why not? Far better a sinless dove sitting upon the branch of a tree, cooing the plaintive song the great Teacher has taught it, than a wicked man with an appalling apprehension of a miserable future and a certain prospect of perdition staring him in the face. Therefore if a man becomes wretched in the future it is his own fault; for he had the opportunity and the power to mount to a glorious state of purity and happiness, and if he neglects these the blame is not upon his Creator.

But on the other hand, if he makes a proper use of his moral powers, and vanquishes, like a Christian hero should, all the trials and difficulties that encompass him, he will have no occasion to murmur at his lot or to envy the future happiness of beings beneath him.

God has decreed that man shall be happy if he will, and the means are placed within his power. If he is ultimately miserable, it is the result of his own unrestrained choice. Therefore God's purposes are fulfilled either in his happiness or misery, because He has purposed that he shall be happy if he will, and that misery shall be the result of his disobedience. But though the lower animals never sinned against God and are involved in the suffering of sinful man without any fault of their own, yet they have no choice or means of correcting their misery. Now, it follows that the Creator, whose " tender mercy is over all His works," and " whose judgment is just," will find some means by which these innocent suffering creatures shall be compensated. That they have no compensation here, their intense suffering, labors, and agonizing deaths prove; and if they are to have any compensation, they must have it in another state of existence. God must have originally designed them for that measure of happiness which is suited to the nature and power He gave them, but they have been deprived of the greater portion by the fall of man and the curse of sin.   It is then obvious that the original purpose of the Creator has not been fulfilled in them and cannot be until they are restored to the primeval happiness they enjoyed before the fall.

Theology teaches that heathen, idiots, and children are saved by reason of the fact that in them the purposes of God have never been fulfilled, and the responsibility for action never reached.   Now is it not a reasonable conclusion that God has provided immortality for animals on the same ground that He has provided it for the heathen, the idiot, and the child ?   Each possesses a corporal structure and a vital and mental organism, and why the Creator of all should decree that one should live forever and the other be doomed to annihilation is a sad problem to solve.   But as mind, or soul, is discernible in the lower animals as well as in man, they probably have the same assurance of immortality.

Sir Benjamin Brodie, of England, says: "The mental principle in animals is of the same essence as that of human beings; so that even in the humbler classes we may trace the rudiments of these faculties to which, in their state of more complete development, we are indebted for the grandest results of human genius. I am inclined to believe that the minds of the inferior animals are essentially of the same nature with that of the human race."

Rev. John Wesley's conclusion as to the nature of the living soul imparted to Adam was that "God gave him such life as other animals enjoy." The inspired writer makes it plain when he says, "Yea, they have all one breath so that a man hath no preëminence above a beast."

When I reflect upon the marred, blackened, sinful disorder of the moral world, and attempt to answer the question as to why innocent animals have to suffer agonizing pain and the tortures of death for the comfort and amusement of man; or why, because of man's sinful disobedience, one animal has to die to furnish food for another, I can only harmonize the matter upon the hypothesis that the infinite goodness and justice of the All-Wise Creator will somewhere and sometime provide a home of eternal rest and happiness for animals. It seems to me Nature teaches this, and justice and mercy demand it.

Whether it is a question as to animals having immortal souls or not, I prefer to stand firm, now and forever, on this question of justice and mercy.

" For right is right, since God is God,
   And right the day must win ;
To doubt would be disloyalty,
   To falter would be sin "

From a humane standpoint, why any Christian
should oppose the theory of the immortality of
animals seems strange to me.   The doctrine is certainly a step higher in the ladder of Christian love
and fellowship.   It adds another reason why Christ
" offered Himself a sacrifice for the sins of the
world," and is in harmony with the history of
God's dealing in the world and the attributes of
the Creator as we have learned them.   It is a mistaken idea, on the part of the Church, to suppose
that it gives greater strength to the evidence for
the immortality of man to ignore the immortality
of lower animals ; for it is less difficult, as I shall
show further on, to convince the scientific world
that all animals have souls than it is to convince
scientists that man alone has a soul.

I cannot see that there was any distinction made
in the original creation, since man and the lower
animals were created out of like primary matter,
and have like organs, and each organ is subject to
like functions.

We see unity in all forms of creation of earth and

heaven, and we see it in animal life. We see evidence of intelligence and goodness in nature, and must conclude that the Author must be intelligent and good.

The word God is synonymous with good, and without His kindness and goodness manifested to His creatures universally, we cannot understand His attributes. "Thy righteousness is like the great mountains; O Lord, Thou preservest man and beast."

CHAPTER IV

THE NEW TESTAMENT ANIMALS' BEST FRIEND —CHRIST AS A HUMANE TEACHER

The relation of Christ to lower animals—Duty of man to follow His example—The folly of sacrifices—Abolished by the Christian dispensation.

I HAVE dwelt at some length on the teachings of the first part of the Bible. I will now endeavor to show wherein the New Testament is animals' best friend. If by the original sin of man all animals were affected in the fall, and if by the atonement of Christ man is affected in the restoration, certainly lower animals are likewise affected. There can be no other reasonable conclusion. Paul says that "Adam was the figure of Him that was to come;" that is, Christ was to be the second Adam. Now, under the first Adam, lower animals were created without death or sin, but fell with man; so in the final destiny they will be restored with man under the second Adam, for "as in Adam all die, so in Christ shall all be made alive." As Christ came into the world as a mediator to restore the fallen condition of man and lower animals, the New Testament becomes the animals' Bible as well as the Christians'. I make this statement with all reverence, for we must admit that the world of reason and justice is a part of the same creation, as the world of matter and sense.

The Hindoos have their Vedas; the Mohammedans their Koran; the Jews their Talmud; the Christians their Bible; and the animals have their consolation and hope of restoration in the teachings of the New Testament.

Christ, in His first sermon, "opened His mouth and said : Blessed are the poor in spirit for theirs is the kingdom of heaven. Blessed are the merciful for they shall obtain mercy." In all God's creation no creatures were so "poor in spirit" as the lower animals, and man cannot have his attention called to a more humane expression than this: "Blessed are the merciful."

Christ's teachings are of the most humane character. No doctrines ever offered to this benighted sin-cursed world have done more to lessen the suffering of animals than His. The pathetic history of our Saviour's life furnishes a beautiful lesson as to the proper relation of man to animals.

Perhaps Christ was born among the cattle, the sheep, the camels, and the dogs, in order that He might, in some way unknown to us, alleviate the condition of poor, forsaken, fallen animals. He recognizes in them qualities similar to His own. He speaks of them as possessing sensitive natures capable of happiness and misery, and therefore enjoins the duty of kindness and mercy towards all living creatures.

Rev. Dr. Talmage in speaking on this subject makes the following beautiful remarks: " Behold in the first place, that on the first night of Christ's life God honored the animal creation. You cannot get into that Bethlehem barn without going past the camels, the mules, the dogs, the oxen. The animals of that stable heard the first cry of the infant Lord. Some of the old painters represent the oxen and camels kneeling that night before the new-born babe. And well might they kneel. Have you ever thought that Christ came, among other things, to alleviate the sufferings of the animal creation? Was it not appropriate that He should, during the first few days and nights of His life on earth, be surrounded by the dumb beasts whose moans and plaint have for ages been a prayer to God for the arresting of their tortures and the righting of their wrongs? It did not merely 'happen so,' that the unintelligent creatures of God should have been that night in close neighborhood. Not a kennel in all the centuries, not a robbed bird's nest, not a worn-out horse on the tow-path, not a herd freezing in the poorly-built cow-pen, not a freight car bringing the beeves to market without water through a thousand miles of agony, not a surgeon's room witnessing the struggles of the fox or rabbit or pigeon or dog in the horrors of vivisection, but has an interest in the fact that Christ was born in a stable surrounded by animals. He remembers that night, and the prayer He heard in their pitiful moan He will answer in the punishment of those who maltreat them."

On many occasions Christ urges their meekness and innocence upon His followers. He compares Himself to an innocent dove and the meek and docile lamb. "I am the door, by Me the sheep enter . . . . He gathereth the lambs in His arms, and carries them in His bosom, and gently leads those that are with young."

The Saviour represents the spirit of kindness in the figure of the Good Shepherd. He tells His hearers that the birds of the air are fed by the Divine Parent, without any provision of labor on their part, and declares that the most insignificant of them does not perish unnoticed by the Creator

His mission on earth was designedly inaugurated by the heavens opening and the Spirit like a dove descending upon Him.

How fitting Christ's mission was to the fallen world is represented by the likeness of one of the innocent and helpless fallen. Christ went about continually doing good in His labor of love and mercy. He had no rest and knew no pleasure but in doing His Father's business, working the work of Him who sent Him, which may all be comprehended in one text, "to seek and to save that which was lost."

His influence should implant a principle in the hearts of His followers, causing them to imitate His example. There are plenty of opportunities We cannot walk abroad without being assailed by the cry of helplessness or without coming into contact with scenes of pain. These send forth an appeal which cannot be misunderstood and ought not to be disregarded. Christ's ready and tender nature pitied and relieved the distressed. He taught mankind to forgive offenses, to commiserate sorrow, and relieve suffering. He commands us to imitate the conduct of the charitable Samaritan, to pity the distress even of an enemy, and to exert our best endeavors for the relief of all suffering.

If we know nothing of the compassion of Jesus, we know nothing of what true compassion is, or of how it has been perfectly and affectionately displayed.

We love and admire the person who pities and helps the afflicted, the distressed, the suffering. We think with delight and exultation of the tender and deep compassion of a Howard, a Brainard, an Elliot, a Nightingale, a Bergh, a Cobbe, an Angell, a Colam, and many others whose names are justly inscribed on the pages of philanthropy. They have been bright ornaments of humanity and friends to the sorrowful and oppressed

But a far more compassionate personage than any of these, or any human being, was the Saviour of the world who set the example for all mankind. This ready and benevolent tendency of His nature, to pity and relieve the miserable, was one of the loveliest features in the character of our Saviour.

He did not appear in the majesty of a sovereign or the glory of a bloody conqueror. He occupied a station not among the princes and potentates of the world, but among the lowly and sorrowful. His birth was even more humiliating and His bodily wants greater than the animals with which He was surrounded, for the foxes had holes and the birds of the air had nests, while the Son of Man had not where to lay His head.

There is another reason why the New Testament is animals' best friend. Christ in offering Himself as a living sacrifice for the sins of the world established the fact that " to do justice and judgment is more acceptable to the Lord than sacrifices "

He is represented as that bright and morning Star which became the Light of the World and gave to mankind a clear and full revelation of the nature and perfections of God and made known the way of reconciliation by offering Himself a living sacrifice for the world and thereby dispensing with any further excuse for that sad rite of offering up animal sacrifices.

How dark and confused were the notions of the philosophers, at the time of the coming of Christ,

on the subject of animal sacrifices! We cannot
find in the Bible a satisfactory reason why it was
first practiced. It did not restore fallen man to his
former holiness nor effect his salvation. If such
had been the case it would not have required the
sacrifice of the Son of God. Some theologians tell
us it was typical of the coming of Christ, but that
part of the Bible written before the coming of
Christ and during the time it was practiced does
not say so. We deny the right to such interpretation. Human reason cannot point out the fitness
or congruity between the slaying of an animal and
the reception by man of pardon for the violation of
God's law.

How the world came to practice sacrifices to
such an extent remains a profound mystery. Long
before the Christian era the Buddhist religion
repudiated the rite and prohibited its use in all the
Orient over which it had influence. Judaism was
the last to give up this sad and cruel ceremony.

It is certain that the wisest heathen philosophers, Pythagoras, Plato, and others, opposed the
doctrine of sacrifice and " wondered how an institution so dismal and so big with absurdity could
diffuse itself through the world." They ridiculed

the idea that the offering of sacrifices could please such a being as a true and living God.

Porphyry says, "We ought then, having been united and made like to God, to offer our own conduct as a holy sacrifice to Him, the same being also a hymn and our salvation in passionless excellence of soul"

It is claimed that the reason it spread so extensively was that the priests who shared with the gods and received the best portion of the meat, were instrumental in urging it on. The early history of sacrifices as practiced by all nations shows that they consisted of fruits, grain, and oil. The sacrifice of living human beings and lower animals was the outgrowth of a depraved cannibal nature and the notion that it was surrounded with greater mystical signification than other sacrifices. These sacrifices were offered to all kinds of imaginary gods and idols with the absurd notion that such gods demanded the life of some innocent being. Hence we find that each deity demanded a particular kind of victim.

One god was known as the "man-eater," another as the "goat-eater," others as the "ram-eater," the "eater of raw flesh," etc. The Persians had one god "who desired nothing but the souls of the victims" The Arabs had one god who was very charitable, and demanded only "half of the blood of victims." The Romans had a carnivorous god "who was wont to eat human flesh."

Some nations believed that by eating the flesh of a victim its life would be renewed in the lives of those who ate it; hence the Issendones would eat their parents and children in order to retain or perpetuate the family.

Another prominent feature of sacrifice was the supposed unity of kinship by mingling the blood of the victim in the veins of the whole tribe. The blood-covenant was formed by eating the same victim and having the same kind of blood course through the veins of all. But if this sacrificial blood was not partaken of it was sprinkled over the people for the same purpose.

Some portions of the Old Testament speak out plainly against sacrifice, thus: "The sacrifices of God are a broken spirit; a broken and a contrite heart. . . . For I spake not unto your fathers nor commanded them in the days that I brought them out of the land of Egypt, concerning burnt offerings or sacrifices. . . . I delight not in the blood of bullocks, or of lambs or of he-goats. . .   If I were hungry, I would not tell thee: for the world is mine, and the fulness thereof. Will I eat the flesh of bulls, or drink the blood of goats? . . . Though you offer me burnt offerings and your meat offerings I will not accept them. . . . For I desire mercy and not sacrifice."

Throughout the Old Testament it was customary when introducing any new law, command, or form of worship, to say "the Lord said" so and so, and thereby many things were put into the Lord's mouth which He undoubtedly never said nor approved.

When the tabernacles or temples or places of worship were mentioned everything was represented as being done for the Lord or in His presence, just as we now call a church the house of the Lord and speak of God's altar within; but in either case it would be a reflection on the omniscience and goodness of God to say that He approved of all that was done and said in His name.

Rev. Dr. Robert Patterson, in his book entitled "Fables of Infidelity," published by the Scriptural Tract Repository, and endorsed by the Church, makes the following appropriate statement: "When we say that God is the Author of the Bible, and that it carries with it a divine authority because it is the Word of God, we do not mean that God is the Author of every saying in it, and that every statement recorded in it is God's mind. Nor when we say that God directed the prophets what to write, and how to write it, do we mean that He also so guided every piece of their behavior, as that they never went wrong"

The clergyman of one church will contend that the Lord commands him to say and do a certain thing, while the clergyman of another church will contend that the Lord commands him to say and do something entirely different.

The fact that a thing is done in the name of the Deity does not make it right if it is not the expressed will of God. We see this illustrated when a Hindoo mother makes a living sacrifice of her infant by throwing it under the wheels of the Juggernaut to be crushed to death in order to appease the supposed wrath of her god; or when the Indians, not a century ago, offered their annual living sacrifice to the Great Father by sending one of their tribe over Niagara Falls in a canoe. The old adage, that believing a thing is right, does not make it so, will apply in this case.

Finally the Christian dispensation has annihilated the sad and repulsive ceremony of animal sacrifices and that for us settles the question.

St. Paul says: " It is not possible that the blood of bulls and of goats should take away sins   In burnt offerings and sacrifices for sin thou hast had no pleasure.   And every priest standeth daily ministering and offering oftentimes the same sacrifice, which can never take away sins."

Now I do not wish to say anything derogatory to the honor of that dispensation which the Almighty for a time, and for a purpose, of which we know but little, permitted; but this much I will say, that even in its best state the Mosaic economy was characterized by obscurity, darkness, and suffering, as compared with the glorious light of the gospel ushered in by Christ who "appeared in the world to put away sin by the sacrifice of Himself."

CHAPTER V

THE BIBLE TEACHES THE IMMORTALITY OF ANIMALS — OPINIONS OF SOME GREAT AUTHORS

God has never ceased to remember and care for all His creatures —St Paul believes in the final redemption of lower animals— Transmigration of souls.

THE undercurrent of Bible history shows conclusively that God has never lost sight of His care and love for the lower animals as well as for man. The language of Scripture everywhere teaches compassion and tenderness towards lower animals. The person who fails to recognize this truth fails to recognize the true meaning and force of some of the most tender and instructive parables and passages of revelation. The qualities, the powers, the beauties of lower animals, are declared to have been specifically given them by the Creator.

All receive their appointed food from Him in due season, and are called upon to praise Him. Kindness to them is inculcated, and cruelty reprobated. The destruction of a wicked city was prohibited for the sake of the lives of lower animals.

In the final state of the world the ferocious and the carnivorous animals will change their destructive appetites and passions. They will eat vegetable food, and become gentle, and exhibit kindly dispositions, and all will be restored to primeval peace and happiness.

There is a current of thought from the beginning to the end of the Bible which either expresses or implies that animals share with man immortal life.

But in order to comprehend this mighty truth we must lay aside prejudice and remember the various translations the Bible has undergone and the indifference of theologians on this subject.

St Paul in his letter to the Romans makes a statement which cannot be interpreted to mean anything else than that animals suffered equally with man in the fall and will be restored through Christ.

St. Paul says: "God having made known unto us the mystery of His will according to His good pleasure, that, in the dispensation of the fulness of time, He might gather together in one all things in Christ both which are in heaven and which are on the earth. . . . For the earnest expectation of the creature waiteth for the manifestation of the sons of God. For the creature was made subject to vanity, not willingly, but by reason of Him who hath subjected the same in hope, because the creature itself also shall be delivered from the bondage of corruption into the glorious liberty of the children of God. For we know that the whole creation groaneth and travaileth in pain together until now. And not only they, but ourselves also, which have the first-fruits of the Spirit, even we ourselves groan within ourselves waiting for the adoption, to wit, the redemption of our body."

Every sentence in the above quotation proves that animals have immortal souls and that they are waiting for the redemption which was made through the atonement of Christ. In the first sentence quoted, when the inspired writer says God will gather together, in one, all things in Christ, both which are in heaven and which are on the earth, He could not possibly limit "all things" to man alone. No man of education would risk his reputation by asserting that man alone was included.

In the next sentence the word creature cannot mean man, for the writer declares that the whole creation groaneth, and not only they, the creatures, but ourselves, man, also.

St. Paul gives us to understand that this suffering of animals shall not be hopeless, but that they shall be delivered together with man from the bondage of corruption By the word creature is understood all living beings except man. He is not here implied, as St. Paul kept men separate in order to make his argument clear. The creature was made subject to vanity, or sin; not willingly, that is, not from choice, but by reason of Him who subjected the same, that is, through Adam, who by his transgression brought the creature into bondage and subjection to the evils of sin. The word creature is used to point out the lower order of beings in contrast with man. They shall be delivered from the bondage of corruption, (that is, from the state of decay which belongs to the matter and not the soul), into the glorious liberty of the children of God; that is, into the same happy condition of freedom and deliverance from the evil, which will be the final privilege of the redeemed.

That the creatures themselves, when this glory is revealed in the sons of God. shall then also be delivered from the bondage of sin, in the final restitution, is plain. The word creature used in the sense of the passage quoted is so very different in its purport from any passage wherein man is referred to that there can be no parallel.[1]

John Wesley, in speaking of a general restoration of all animal life, says: "Nothing can be more plainly expressed. Away with vulgar prejudice and let the plain Word of God take its place. They (the animals) shall be delivered from the bondage of corruption into glorious liberty, even a measure, according as they are capable, of the liberty of the children of God. A general view of that is given in the eighth chapter of Romans. Then the following blessing shall be given, not only to the children of men, for there is no such restriction in the text, but to every creature according to its capacity: 'God shall wipe away all tears

---

[1] There is a plain distinction made by using in contrast the words *creature* and *they* with *man* and *ourselves*. It is a plain observation from nature, as well as revelation, that every inferior creature in the universe travails in pain, and not only they, but we ourselves, we of the human species, groan within ourselves, waiting for the redemption of our bodies from the evils they now labor under. The creatures or lower animals were made subject to vanity or sin "through our offense," and groan under the curse of man's disobedience, but in due time these poor creatures shall be delivered from the bondage of corruption and be restored along with man to happiness. There shall be a "restoration of all things as God hath promised by the mouth of all His holy prophets," when the new heaven and the new earth are to be inhabited.

from their eyes, and there shall be no more death, neither sorrow nor crying; neither shall there be any more pain: for the former things are passed away' What if it should then please the All-Wise and All-Gracious Creator to raise the creatures, which we now call inferior animals, to a higher grade in the scale of creation? What if it should please Him, in the great regeneration, when He makes us 'equal to the angels,' to make them what we are now? Thus in that day all the vanity to which they are now helplessly subject will be abolished; they will suffer no more, either from within or without; the days of their groaning will be ended. In the new earth as well as the new heavens, there will be nothing to give pain, but everything that the wisdom and goodness of God can create to give happiness. As a recompense for what they once suffered while under the 'bondage of corruption,' when God has 'renewed the face of the earth' and their corruptible bodies have put on incorruption, they shall enjoy happiness, suited to their state, without alloy, without interruption, and without end."

Rev. Dr. Edward B. Pusey says that "all nature, having suffered together, shall be restored together.

As to us, death is to be the gate of immortality and glory, so in some way to them creation includes all created beings, and all creation must include our nature too, in that one common groan and pang."

The great philosopher and theologian, Bishop Butler, says: "We cannot argue from the reason of the thing that death is the destruction of living agents. Neither can we find anything in the whole analogy of nature to afford us even the slightest presumption that animals ever lose their living powers; much less, if it were possible, that they lose them by death. The immortality of brutes does not necessarily imply that they are endowed with any latent capacities of a rational or moral nature. The economy of the universe might require that there should be immortal creatures without any capacities of this kind."

Canon Wilberforce, in an eloquent speech before a meeting of the Anti-Vivisection Society in London said he believed that "these beautiful and useful forms of life, which are sometimes so cruelly tortured, are bound to pass over into another sphere, and that in the great eternal world men and animals should sink or swim together."

Rev. Joseph Cook says: "Do not facts require us

to hold that the immortal part in animals having
higher than automatic endowments is external to
the nervous mechanism in them as well as in man?
What are we to say if we find that straightforward-
ness may lead us to the conclusion that Agassiz
was not unjustifiable when he affirmed, in the name
of science, that instinct may be immortal, and
when he expressed, in his own name, the ardent
hope that it might be so. Shall we, too, not hope
that this highest conception of paradise may be the
true one? Would it not be a diminution of supreme bliss not to have union with God through
these, the most majestic of His works below ourselves?"

Agassiz, the greatest scientist we ever have had
on this continent, and a man of profound religious
convictions, was a firm believer in some future life
for lower animals. He says: "Most of the arguments of philosophy in favor of the immortality of
man apply equally to the permanency of the immortal principle in other living beings. May I not
add that a future life in which man should be
deprived of that great source of enjoyment, and
intellectual and moral improvement, which result
from the contemplation of the harmonies of an

organic world, would involve a lamentable loss; and may we not look to a spiritual concert of the combined worlds and all their inhabitants in the presence of their Creator, as the highest conception of paradise? In some incomprehensible way, God Almighty has created these beings, and I cannot doubt of their immortality any more than I doubt of my own "

Rev. Dr. Adam Clark, one among the greatest theologians of his day, makes the following plain and unmistakable statement: " It does not appear that the animal creation are capable of a choice; and it is evident that they are not placed in their present misery, through either their choice or their sin; and if no purpose of God can be ultimately frustrated these creatures must be restored to that state of happiness for which they have been made, and of which they have been deprived through the transgression of man. Had not sin entered into the world, they would have had much greater enjoyments, without pain, excessive labor, and toil, and without death, and all those sufferings which arise from the fall. It is therefore obvious that the gracious purpose of God has not been fulfilled in them; and that, as they have not lost their

happiness through their own fault, both the beneficence and justice of God are bound to make them a
reparation. Hence it is reasonable to conclude
that, as from the present constitution of things
they cannot have the happiness designed for them
in this state, they must have it in another."

Mrs. Mary Somerville, who was a member of the
philosophical societies and academies of science
both in England and Germany, and who was noted,
the world over, for her scientific knowledge and
womanly virtues, when speaking on the subject of
death, said: "I shall regret the sky, the sea, with
all the changes of their beautiful coloring; the
earth, with its verdure and flowers: but far more
shall I grieve to leave animals who have followed
our steps affectionately for years, without knowing
for certain their ultimate fate, though I firmly
believe that the living principle is never extinguished. I am sincerely happy to find that
I am not the only believer in the immortality of
the lower animals."

Miss Frances Power Cobbe, of England, a noted
writer, says: "I will venture to say plainly that, so
far as appears to me, there is no possible solution
of this heart-wearing question save the bold as-

sumption that the existence of animals does not
end at death. It is absolutely necessary to postu-
late a future life for the tortured dog or cat or
horse or monkey, if we would escape the un-
bearable conclusion that a sentient creature, un-
offending, nay, incapable of giving offense, has
been given by the Creator an existence which, on
the whole, has been a curse. That conclusion
would be blasphemy. Rejecting it with all the
energy of our souls, we find ourselves logically
driven to assume the future life of lower animals."

Rev. J. G. Wood, author of "Man and Beast,"
says: "I feel sure that animals will have the opportunity of developing their latent faculties in the
next world, though their free scope has been denied
to them in the short time of their existence in the
present world. They surpass many human beings
in love, unselfishness, generosity, conscience, and
self-sacrifice. I claim for them a higher status in
creation than is generally attributed to them, and
claim they have a future life in which they can be
compensated for the suffering which so many of
them have to undergo in this world. I am quite sure
that most of the cruelties which are perpetrated on
animals are due to the habit of considering them as

mere machines, without susceptibilities, without reason, and without the capacity of a future."

George T. Angell, President of the American Humane Education Society, and a noted humanitarian, says, "Can there be any doubt that the Almighty, who has given them (animals) one life, has power, if He wishes, to give them another? In God's great universe, comprising as it does perhaps millions of worlds larger than our own, is there not room enough for all?"

Rev. Canon I T. Carter, a noted English clergyman, says: "We may, moreover, connect with the resurrection of our Lord, the hope for restoration of the entire creation; for the whole world looks forward to that future state. As the whole world of creation around us suffers from the effect of the fall, so in some way they will know a resurrection, and be transformed into a pure, more blessed, more beautiful, state. The lowest creatures are not to be destroyed, but after their manner, according to their kind, will be restored, giving praise and glory to 'Him who created them'"

Rev. Robert Eyton makes the following beautiful remarks: "To some of us it would be a great sorrow to think that after this life we are forever entirely and hopelessly separated from that animal world in which many of the deepest of our interests are to be found   It would seem strange to us to think that man should have this world as his home, and should form those wonderful and beautiful relations with many of the animals below him that he now does, and then afterwards, in the new earth, these relations should cease, and that God is then to be looked on henceforth as the God of human beings only, and not of the animal creation But when we think of animals as being objects of God's creative love, it at once puts us in a new relation towards them and gives us a new hope about their future."

Rev H Kirby, of England, says: "We are led to conclude that the suffering, violence, and death which animals have to endure, either at the hand of man or of other animals, did not exist until after the fall of man, and that therefore they are one of the consequences of sin. In other words, the lower animals, who themselves are not guilty of any sin, are nevertheless, undergoing a share of the punishment due to man's sin

"This would lead us to suppose, from what we know of God's goodness, justice, and equity, that if

guilty men are to enjoy the benefits of Christ's In-
carnation and Atonement, and are to receive much
more than an equivalent for their miseries and suffering, then innocent animals may in all reason
look for some recompense for all the ills which
they now endure: and since there seems to be but
little alleviation of their troubles in the present life,
we infer that it may take place in a future and immortal life, of which they are capable from their
twofold nature of body and soul."

Dr. John Fulton, of New York, a clergyman
of deep piety and bright intellect, recently made
the following statement: "This is a redeemed
world, with not one suffering creature that has
been left out of Christ's all-embracing redemption.
And more, I dare believe that St. Paul was right
when he looked upon this redeemed world, and seeing how its lower orders are groaning and suffering
together with us, even until now, he was inspired
to prophesy of a better time, when their redemption and ours shall be perfected together, and the
glory that is to be revealed shall surpass all the
present suffering. My own belief is that, in some
way, which I do not pretend to understand, but in
which I can nevertheless believe, the salvation of

Christ is broad enough to include and does include the dumb creation."

But one could continue to mention hundreds of noted divines, authors, and scientists, of modern times, as well as ancient writers, who have expressed themselves as believing in the immortality of animals. The doctrine was maintained by a large majority of ancient philosophers, though like the immortality of man, it was of a very uncertain and crude nature.

The old school of Platonists claimed that the souls of all living creatures were a part of the universal soul of the world, and that they were depressed or immerged in the animal body, and when the body died the soul would go to some other living being, sometimes to a man and sometimes to a lower animal.

This doctrine of the transmigration of souls, crude as it was, shows a noble and humane device of the ancients to deter men from indulging in sordid and mean passions. To teach that the souls of men after their separation from the body should pass into the form of such animals as they most resembled in their dispositions, then to endure the horrors and suffering which they were guilty of inflicting, was a wholesome doctrine in those dark days

If the souls of some of our two-legged animals who have wantonly abused and tortured so many of the quadrupeds should be transmigrated into their forms long enough to realize the regions of hell they have made for them on earth, the angels of mercy would undoubtedly shout, amen!

Menander, a Greek writer, speaking on the subject of transmigration, said to Crato, "When you die you will have a second existence; therefore choose what creature you would like to be, dog, sheep, goat, horse, or man." To which he replied, "Make me anything rather than a man, for he is the only creature that prospers by injustice." Though this was spoken many hundred years ago, yet it is a lamentable fact that it has lost none of its truth.

The doctrine of the immortality of animals was maintained by many Jewish writers and a long list of ancient Christian writers could be mentioned.

Manasseh, a noted Jewish Rabbi, in his discourse on the resurrection, asserts that "dumb animals will have a much happier state than they ever enjoyed here when they with man shall rise again."

And Philo, in his book of future rewards, speaks as follows: "There is no doubt but that hereafter dumb animals will be divested of their ferocity, and become tame and gentle after the manner of other creatures whose dispositions are subdued to harmony and love."

Tertullian, a noted Christian writer, makes the following remarks: "There shall be an end of death, when the devil, its chief master, shall go away into the fire which God has prepared for him and his angels; when the manifestations of the sons of God shall release the world from evil, at present universally subject to it; when the innocence and purity of nature being restored, animals shall live in harmony with each other, and infants shall play without harm with animals once ferocious; when the Father shall have subdued His enemies to His Son and put all things in subjection under His feet."

CHAPTER VI

ANIMALS PROMISED A PARADISE — COMMANDED TO PRAISE THEIR CREATOR

Animals to be restored to primeval peace and happiness—Are seen in heaven—Two passages of Scripture usually not properly interpreted.

In the promise of a new heaven and a new earth God has given a plain revelation to man of the restoration of all animals. In this new Garden of Eden all things are to be restored to their former harmony; there will be perpetual peace and happiness, and all shall dwell together in love. The animal creation shall again gladden a new Paradise as they did when Adam and Eve called them by name, and caressed them and mingled in their society.

The Bible everywhere indicates that the new earth will be a counterpart of the old before the fall, so we must conclude that lower animals, who were created before man and have been his companions before and since the fall, will be restored with him in the "new creation." The inspired writer Isaiah, looking beyond the present suffering and disorganized condition of animals, declares that the time will come when "the wolf shall dwell with the lamb, and the leopard shall lie down with the kid; the calf and the young lion and the fatling together; and a little child shall lead them. And the cow and the bear shall feed; their young ones shall lie down together, and the lion shall eat straw like the ox. And the sucking child shall play on the hole of the asp, and the weaned child shall put his hand on the cockatrice's den. They shall not hurt nor destroy in all My holy mountain; for the earth shall be full of the knowledge of the Lord, as the waters cover the sea."

This description of the inspired writer fully portrays the condition which existed in the Garden of Eden before the fall, and shows conclusively that the same relation will again exist among the animals, and that God has created or prepared a new world for them; or, as St. Paul says: "In the dispensation of the fulness of time Christ might gather together in one *all things* in Him, both which are in the heavens and which are on the earth; even in Him"

St. Peter says, "And God shall send Jesus

Christ, which before was preached unto you, whom the heaven must receive until the times of restitution of all things. For according to His promise, we look for new heavens and a new earth."

Now if all things are to be restored, animals are to be restored; and if this whole material system is to be renewed, does not this include the material forms of all living creatures?

When lower animals were made to suffer for man's sin at the time of the flood, God made a promise to them as well as to man that such a thing should never occur again, in these words. "I will remember My covenant, which is between Me and you and every living creature of all flesh; and the waters shall no more become a flood to destroy all flesh." Why should God include in His covenant lower animals if they were not immortal as well as man, and were not to share alike a future destiny?

Had not Satan interfered to mar the harmony between man and animals in the original Paradise, they would still be living in the bonds of a holy and happy fellowship without sin or suffering.

To doubt that God will restore this happy fellowship would be to deny that it ever did exist and to deny the plain teachings of the Bible and all the good and great attributes of our Heavenly Father.

Isaiah, in speaking of the "restitution of all things," says: "In that day shall the cattle feed in large pastures. The oxen likewise and the young asses that ear the ground shall eat clean provender, which hath been winnowed with the shovel and with the fan." Then again, if there was to be no future state for lower animals, why does God call on them to praise Him? If the Creator made them "very good," without being capable of sin, and through man's disobedience they have to suffer with him the curse of the fall, it would seem like mockery to call upon them to praise Him if they are to be doomed to an eternal annihilation

God says in His revealed word, "Let the heavens and earth praise Him. . . . Beasts, and all cattle; creeping things and flying fowls. . . . Let everything that hath breath praise the Lord."

St. John the Divine, who represents himself as speaking through "The Revelation of Jesus Christ," gives us to understand that there are lower animals as well as man in heaven, and that they all give praise unto the Lord. He says he

saw four beasts together with twenty-four elders
who were near the throne of God, and that these
"beasts gave glory and honor and thanks to Him
that sat on the throne." And further on he relates
that he saw in heaven, horses, sheep, leopards, lions,
frogs, fowls, birds, and insects; that the beasts
consisted of tens of thousands; and that " every
creature which is in heaven and on the earth and
under the earth, and such as are in the sea and all
that are in them, heard I saying, Blessing and
honor and glory and power be unto Him that
sitteth upon the throne. . . . Thou art worthy,
O Lord, to receive glory and honor and power; for
Thou hast created all things, and for Thy pleasure
they are and were created." If lower animals " are
and were " created for His pleasure, it must be in
the future state, for it certainly could not be in accordance with the nature of the Creator, to take
pleasure in the terrible suffering they have to endure in this world.

It is very obvious that when " God saw everything that He had made, and, behold, it was very
good," He was looking through and beyond the
intermediate state to the ultimate purpose of creation There is no other way to solve this sad,

perplexing question, and no other reason why God
would call on lower animals to praise Him. When
we hear Christian people sing that beautiful verse
composed by Bishop Thomas Ken:

"Praise God from whom all blessings flow,
Praise Him *all creatures* here below,"

we wonder if they really comprehend its true import. No doubt the great and good bishop was sincere when he composed that grand doxology which
will be sung as long as the Christian Church is per-
petuated upon earth; but no man has a moral right
to ask poor, sinless, suffering animals to praise God
unless he feels assured that they will receive a
future recompense for the sad condition man has
brought upon them.

"He prayeth well, who loveth well,
Both man, and bird, and beast.
He prayeth best who loveth best
All things both great and small;
For the great God who loveth us,
He made and loveth all."

While the Bible as clearly conveys the idea that
lower animals are in heaven as it does that men
are in heaven, yet I do not urge this fact as

an argument for the immortality of animals, for God may see fit to give them a separate "country" as He did before the creation of man.

It might be well in this connection to notice briefly the doctrine taught by religions other than Christianity.

The evidence is positive that a belief in an endless existence of lower animals, as well as man, has been maintained throughout the history of man from the creation to the present time. Thousands of years before the Christian era, the Egyptians show evidence of being a highly cultured people in morals, art, literature, and the sciences. They could build temples, erect massive obelisks, and showed evidence of wonderful attainments in mathematics, engineering, and astronomy. They were, at an early age, more advanced than either the Greeks or the Romans

In the British Museum are sculptured figures in hieroglyphic writing, which can be easily read, that date back as far as 3500 B. C.

In their religious symbolism they show that they were firm believers in the immortality of animals. The large number of animal mummies which are found beside human beings go to show that they placed man and lower animals on an equality so far as future destiny was concerned.

Many animals have special significance in the religious teachings of the Egyptians. The sacred bull, called Apis, was kept in Memphis and treated with great reverence. When one died he was embalmed and buried in a granite sarcophagus in the neighborhood of the Pyramids with a suitable inscription carved on a stone. On one, which is a sample of many, are found the following words: "In the twentieth year, the month Mesori, the twentieth day, under the reign of King Psamethik I, the Majesty of the living Apis departed to heaven."

The Mahometans advocate the doctrine that there is a Paradise, or "Garden of Abode," beneath the seventh heaven and near the throne of God, which is the future abode of the righteous, and that there "there shall be beasts to ride on, ready saddled and bridled and adorned with rich trappings, which will gallop at great speed. Birds shall sing from the branches of the great tuba (tree of happiness)."

Every nation which has attained to any degree of culture has had some sort of religion; and in almost every instance where man has been considered immortal, lower animals have been so considered for the same reasons.

The religions of Egypt and Phœnicia, Islamism, Brahmanism, Zoroastrianism, Buddhism, Greek and Norse religions, Lao-tseism and Confucianism, Judaism from which descended Christianity, and in America the religions of the Peruvians and the Aztecs,—indeed all the primitive religions of the world, directly or indirectly advocate the immortality of lower animals. In many religions of a more crude form, such as we find among the Indians, they too believe that wherever the departed soul of man goes, his faithful horse, dog, wife, and attendants follow.

As heaven is a real place or a world made into a paradise for the abode of man, so the Creator has provided somewhere in His numerous systems of worlds a place for all animals, as I show further on

This is certainly a consistent conclusion from our knowledge of Divine goodness and justice. Instead of limiting the power and goodness of God, I would extend it, not only to the material things we see, but into the vastness of the mysterious immensity of space beyond our view or present comprehension, into myriads of worlds He has in reserve for His purposes.

Instead of circumscribing the Christian religion to one species of God's creatures, I would let its wings of mercy spread out over all suffering animal life. It is a narrow conclusion to suppose that man is the only animal the Creator has provided for or cares for. The place man holds in comparison with the universe is humble beyond all statement of degree.

There are angels, archangels, cherubim, seraphim, and various other spirits in the celestial hierarchy which are as far above man as the heavens are above the earth How unreasonable to believe that the Creator, who made the lower animals and endowed them with a high sense of enjoyment, turned them out into the wide theatre of the universe, there to struggle as best they could, and to endure all the suffering and torture their sensitive, quivering nerves could bear ; and then doomed them to an eternal annihilation. Would such a partial destiny be consistent with the attributes of a Christian's God ? We look at the low and degraded state of the Hindoos, the Hottentots, the Bushmen, and ask the question, " How is it possible that these can live again?" We look into the bright liquid eyes of an intelligent lower animal and ask the same question. The following question was asked over nineteen hundred years ago, and is still being asked: "Why should it be thought a thing incredible with you that God should raise the dead?" and the answer comes from the same volume of revelation: "For as in Adam all die even so in Christ shall all be made alive . . . the tender mercy of God is over all His works . . . in whose hand is the soul of every living thing."

When the world recognizes the solemn truth that all God's creatures are descendants from the same First Cause, that they need the same elements for the support of their bodies; that all are members of the same great community and family; that all are fellow-travelers in the same weary pilgrimage; that all are subject to the same sin, sorrow, pain, and death, as the result of the fall; that all have the same desire for happiness and tenacity for life; and that all possess the same kind of immortality,—then we will have a nucleus around which to gather the grand facts of a humane system of theology.

The passages of Scripture used as arguments against the future existence of lower animals are commonly limited to two, but these when rightly interpreted fail to form a conclusive argument against the immortality of animals.

Solomon, in one of his despondent moods, ironically asks the question, "Who knoweth the spirit of a man that goeth upward, and the spirit of a beast that goeth downward to the earth?" This is as much as to say that such a doctrine might be taught, but who knows it, or would dare advocate it? We can, with like propriety, propound the same question to-day: who knows it? And the answer should be, no one. Solomon did not say he knew it or that he believed it.

Theologians insist that a passage of Scripture must be interpreted by the preceding and following passages and by the context of the whole idea intended. By reading the two passages preceding the one quoted, it can be proven conclusively that the question was ironically asked and that Solomon believed that animals shared alike the same future condition as man. If immortality is the lot of one, it is of all; as they are composed of like dust and have the same breath. Solomon says: "That which befalleth the sons of men befalleth beasts; as the one dieth, so dieth the other; yea, they have all one breath; so that a man hath no preeminence above a beast.   All go to one place."

Again, if the objector will notice the important fact that Solomon here fully recognizes that animals have "spirits" or souls the same as man, we presume he will not consider the quotation so valuable against the immortality of animals.

The other passage urged as an objection against a continuance of the being of lower animals is as futile as the one just noticed   David, in speaking of the rich and wicked man, says: "Nevertheless man being in honor abideth not; he is like the beasts that perish."

In justice to the cause of suffering animals, let us say that this text also is wrongly translated.   It is another instance of the persistent efforts of translators to exclude the lower animals from the benefits of the correct words of revelation

There is no word in the original Hebrew, in the passage referred to, which can be properly translated "perish."   The true translation should be, "like dumb beasts" or "like irrational beasts." The word "perish" does not occur in the original Hebrew and should not be added.   The Jewish Bible, which retains the purest Hebrew, uses the words "like the beasts that are irrational."

The words in the Septuagint were translated "senseless cattle" and in the Wycliffe Bible, were translated "unwise beasts." One of the accepted translations of the Roman Catholic Church of England uses the words "senseless beasts" The word "perish" should not be used. But we will take the English translation as it reads and show that the doctrine of the annihilation of lower animals was not here intended and that the passage says nothing more about the perishing of beasts than other passages do of man. When we read the context it is plain that it has but one meaning; namely, that the rich and wicked man may perish or die and his name be forgotten like a beast which dies and is forgotten. We are aware that lower animals die and perish from our memory, that is, are forgotten, and man is very properly compared to them. Whilst he lives he may be honored for his wealth, notwithstanding he may be mean and insignificant; but when he dies his honor dies with him, and, like a poor, obscure, nameless animal, sinks into oblivion so far as this world is concerned. But the word "perish" does not in any sense mean annihilation, for if it did there would be no future for any but the righteous, which is not in accordance with the teaching of the Bible.

Christ says, " All shall come forth, they that have done good and they that have done evil," and Paul says, " We must all appear before the judgment-seat of Christ."

The word " perish " in the passage referred to is applied to both man and beast alike, and if it means annihilation to one it does to the other.

But it is perfectly plain that it has reference to the memory of man after death and not to his future life. Though a man may have riches and honor yet his name may not abide after death, for he may be forgotten and his name perish like the memory of the beast. Such passages of Scripture are often read without giving them a careful consideration.

In the last verse of the same chapter is a repetition of the same idea with the additional words " understandeth not," which clinches the argument that the comparison of man and lower animals was with reference to the memory of them after death

If the words should be so interpreted as to mean the annihilation of animals, there are scores of passages which would annihilate man by the same argument. I will quote a few from the many. Isaiah says, "Therefore hast thou visited and destroyed them, and made all their memory to perish." Job says, "They are destroyed from morning to evening; they perish forever." In Ecclesiastes we find the following passage: "For the living know that they shall die, but the dead know not anything, neither have they any more a reward, for the memory of them is forgotten. All go unto one place, all are of the dust, and all turn to dust again."

David tells us that "the dead praise not the Lord, neither any that go down into silence. . . . He seeth that wise men die, likewise the fool and the brutish person perish." St. Peter, in speaking of the wicked, says, "They shall be cut down like grass and wither as the green herb."

When Christ and His disciples were out in a ship, a severe storm arose, and the disciples went to Christ and said, "Lord save us: we perish." St. Peter, in speaking of the wicked, says, "They understand not, and shall utterly perish in their own corruption." All such passages refer to the suspension of the corporal powers and not to the spiritual nature of man and lower animals, and certainly Solomon could have had no other idea in view. There is no passage in the Bible so often and so erroneously quoted.

CHAPTER VII

NATURAL THEOLOGY —PHILOSOPHY OF THE SOUL

The lower animals have souls for the same reason that mankind have souls—Scientific reasons for believing in the immortality of animals—Materialism and immaterialism.

WHILE the Bible fully declares the immortality of animals, natural theology just as fully substantiates the same fact. One thing, however, is certain: if the immortality of animals cannot be demonstrated, the contrary cannot. To say that when a house has fallen and is in ruins, it once had an inhabitant, and that he escaped out of it and lives in some other place, can involve no contradiction; but to say that the soul of an animal, when it leaves the body, has found a new and better place, may involve a question. There are some things readily admitted, without an argument, while other things cannot be impressed upon the mind without being analyzed and presented in a logical form.

I attempt to prove by plain and simple propositions that if men have souls lower animals have souls for the same reasons, and that the soul is not only immaterial but that it is immortal, and is a thing separate from the body. Every species of being and every immaterial substance must belong to some region or state, because it must be somewhere and somehow. There is no waste in creation, and everything, however grand or insignificant, was made for some worthy object. It is true such objects may be perverted by the interference of man, but the ultimate good intended will be reached. Nature teaches us to draw conclusions from what we see and know as to the character of things we do not see nor positively know.

Matter is a thing we can see, and we can therefore know something of its properties. We know that by itself it is of a lifeless, inert, and passive nature. But the soul has a freedom to act independently of the laws which govern matter. Mind may be considered as manifesting itself through a series of material organs, although it is totally unlike any of those principles or functions that are termed material, and in fundamental contrast to them. When a man communicates his ideas to an animal it must be through a spiritual medium, for matter or material substance cannot communicate with the soul or immaterial essence; consequently animals must have an immaterial nature or soul the same as man.

This is illustrated in the communication between Balaam and his ass. Balaam mounted his ass and started to fight the Israelites, against God's command, but an angel was sent to warn him to go no farther lest he would be slain. The angel appeared standing in the road with uplifted sword, and was seen by the ass before Balaam's eyes were opened The ass turned aside which so enraged Balaam that he commenced to beat her with his staff. He did not try to find the cause for the ass's fright. "And the Lord opened the mouth of the ass, and she said unto Balaam, What have I done unto thee, that thou hast smitten me these three times? And Balaam said unto the ass, Because thou hast mocked me; I would there were a sword in my hand, for now would I kill thee." The poor ass tried to explain her fright and said, "Am not I thine ass upon which thou hast ridden ever since I was thine unto this day; was I ever wont to do so unto thee?"

While this conversation was going on, Balaam looked up and saw the angel standing in the road, and now it was his turn to apologize to the ass for his hasty cruelty.

The moving agent in this case operated through an immaterial medium upon the donkey as well as upon the man.

Elijah, the prophet, was a good man, and, for reproving the sins of King Ahab, his life was in danger; so the Lord said to him, "Hide thyself by the brook Cherith. I have commanded the ravens to feed thee there." How could it be possible for the ravens to understand this command unless they had souls or an immaterial nature to communicate with a like nature?

Jonah was thrown overboard from a ship by his enemies, but the Lord had in readiness a great fish which was commanded to swallow him, and in three days "the Lord spake unto the fish and it vomited out Jonah upon dry land."

Daniel was cast into the den of lions by King Darius for worshiping the Lord, and he said, "God sent an angel and shut the lions' mouths that they have not hurt me." An angel told the lions not to harm Daniel and they obeyed his command.

Nothing but an immaterial principle within could hear and obey the direct command of an immaterial nature like God or His angels.

If the material organism of animals comes from

matter, then it must be obvious that the mental and vital organism which pervades every living being must come from the immaterial attributes of the Creator, and is eternal. It is claimed by the Church that man is immortal because he can communicate with God. We take the same Bible and prove that God communicated with lower animals, which would indicate a divine nature in them for the same reason.

If an animal moves itself, it does so for some reason and with respect to some end, which is not like material motion which cannot take place only from without by external causes. You cannot imagine matter moved by its own reason. Animals move themselves not only by their own reason, but by reason imparted by signs or words from others. Such motions cannot be the result of the mere physical effects of signs or words, for they would have the same effect whether they were understood or not. It is the soul which interprets the sense of the signs and words and thus causes action, and it is the soul which imparts the principles of life and brings vitality to the body. As long as the soul remains in the body it has the power to move it at will, or otherwise it would be moved by only the laws of gravitation and mechanism.

The immaterial essence of force is the propelling power of the soul.   Animal life is maintained by the Divine will manifested through the law of force, consequently no living being without the aid of some vital force superior to chemical and mechanical forces can live.   Vital force constitutes the phenomena of life, and is entirely distinct from lifeless matter which is devoid of any motion or force except as applied to it from external causes.

Scientists agree that force is an immaterial essence, and forms a substantial entity which is indestructible.   Now everything which is immaterial forms an attribute of God and must be immortal. Force is an immaterial principle and consequently vital-force, mental-force and all other faculties of the soul must be immortal.

It requires force to produce motion, and life is motion, both of which cannot be annihilated, but only changed.

We have, to-day, two classes of scientists who differ widely on biological and psychological science. One class attempts to account for everything that takes place in the body on chemical or mechanical principles, and thus denies the existence of external or soul energy.   It assumes that there is but one substance, and regards mind as but a property or particular manifestation of matter. The other class contends that behind the pressure which produces the motions and sensations of animals is a spiritual nature called soul; and that the material and the mental nature may be regarded from a dualistic point of view as a perfectly distinct kind of reality.

The greater number of modern scientists adopt the latter scientific hypothesis, and contend that the soul is external to the nervous mechanism which it sets in motion, and that there is an external agent in all animal life independent of the body. It is an easy matter, when considering the two schools of philosophy, to see where modern materialism and theology separate. I have for many years been investigating both sides of the question and am thoroughly convinced that life, or the power which gives motion and sensation, must come from without, and is independent of the nervous mechanism; and from this life potency proceeds organization, for there cannot be life without organization to receive it.

The cause of vital movement must exist before the movement. Nothing can exist in an effect which did not previously exist in the cause.

Therefore if life existed before organization, it could certainly exist outside and after dissolution.

When the soul is disengaged from the gross matter, which now incloses and encumbers it, may it not become veiled in its own fine vehicle and, being freed from the laws governing the body, assume the laws which govern the immaterial universe and be conveyed to some prepared state or place of future abode ?

It is a sad fact that there are many mysteries which cluster around this abstruse subject and remain locked in the bosom of the Creator, and are as inscrutable to the sage as to the savage ; to the philosopher as to the schoolboy. No doubt they are hidden for a purpose, and what little we can know of this great cosmos should convince us of man's ignorance and weakness when compared with the great First Cause of all things.

A chemist may decompose blood, gelatine, bone or any constituent part of the body, but he cannot reform one of them. The vital laws, or organic forces, form compounds which can never be produced by chemical affinity. He can no more make a piece of bone than he can make a diamond. It requires a higher intelligence than that of a finite or earthly nature to form the body, and it requires a higher power than matter to operate it when it is formed. How a molecule or protoplasm which forms the germinal matter can produce a bone, tendon, muscle, nerve, or any constituent element of animal life, and change dead matter into a living body, can only be accounted for by recognizing the wisdom and power of the Creator of all things in the initial movement.

According to the teachings of modern philosophy, matter and mind form the only constituent elements of the universe, and as mind is synonymous with soul it would be proper to say that matter and soul are the only constituents of the universe; though there seems to be considerable confusion about the different terms used to express the immaterial part of the body.

A true definition of the nature of the soul is that it consists of a certain simple unextended, indivisible substance, the natural properties whereof are life, understanding, and activity. It is a thing which differs essentially from all material substances; for matter is something, under all forms, which is naturally compounded, extended and divisible; has color, length, breadth, thickness; is hard or soft, rough or smooth, and without understanding and power of motion.

A soul is of contrary nature, and must be uncompounded, unextended, indivisible and whose properties are life, understanding, and activity.

It is that mysterious essence which thinks, moves, and controls the body. Now according to this definition of the essential properties of the soul, it would appear that it is a God-given principle to all living beings, and includes a capacity for immortality and endless duration of existence. As life is the natural property of the soul, and this life property is an attribute of God, we cannot but conceive it as immortal. No supposition can be formed of the destruction of this principle of life, but involves the destruction of this soul nature and essence; because the endless duration of the soul is asserted in its unity, and indivisibility, and because, since having no parts, it cannot be divided into parts, and as a substance uncompounded, it is not liable to dissolution, therefore the soul, truly is a living substance, which cannot perish with the body.

Now, since all beings which have life have souls, and as life is soul, and all souls are immortal and capable of existence forever, nothing therefore can possibly preclude the souls of animals from that perpetual state to come but a fundamental destruction, for they must continue through all revolutions of future ages, unless the Creator who made them shall see fit to doom them to annihilation.

That the soul is endowed with a capacity for a state of separate existence after the death of the corporal frame to which it is attached is a conclusion clearly deduced from both revealed and natural theology.

The brain, being the centre of the nervous system, is the seat of the soul and is the instrument which is employed in all its operations. Though the soul is not matter, yet it works through the means of matter. We say that the eye sees, but the eye cannot see, it is the mere instrument of vision, and is no more to a man than a telescope or microscope. The ear is not hearing, but the organ of hearing; so the brain is not soul, but the organ of the soul by which it works through its different faculties.

To illustrate, I say to a boy, " John, please go and drive the chickens from the garden." He obeys me and then returns feeling proud of having done me a favor. The chickens soon return, so I call my dog and say, "Carlo, go and drive the chickens from the garden." He, also, cheerfully obeys my command, and then returns looking wistfully into my face, as much as to say, "I am glad to obey you and make myself useful." They both suddenly die and lie before me. I look into their faces and see the eyes that guided their bodies; the ears which heard my voice; the limbs which propelled their bodies, and the head which contained the brain over which the soul presided The organs are all there as they were but without life. Now what is life? It is that period during which the body and soul are united. They are not now united; the souls which were behind the nerve systems which caused them to perform those acts have left their bodies. Now what system of logic will sustain the hypothesis that you can call the brain energy in the boy one thing and in the dog another? If that mysterious substance called soul was the cause of action in the one case it was in the other. What has become of that substance which gave motion and sensation to those bodies?

If the mental powers and vital essence of that faithful, intelligent, and confiding dog, with its memory and loving devotion can be annihilated or sink into nonentity at death, what philosophical proof or probable evidence can be adduced to show that the boy shall live after the death of the body? There has been no change in the constituent parts of man and animals since the creation, and what we find now is the same that the Creator first gave to each.

Scientists who advocate the theory of organic evolution admit that all the germs of all the moral and mental faculties of man are contained in the lower animals, and that the vital force, the Bible term for which is soul, is as much a part of lower animals as of man.

Huxley says: "I hold that the nature of the physical and mental faculties of brutes applies in its fulness and entirety to man. The consciousness possessed by lower animals is that sort of consciousness which we have ourselves, and foreshadows more or less those feelings which are possessed by mankind."

Darwin says: "The sense, intuitions and various emotions and faculties of which man boasts, may be found in an incipient or even sometimes in a well-developed condition in the lower animals."

Büchner says: "The standpoint of modern

thought no longer recognizes man and lower animals a difference of kind, but only a difference of degree, and sees the principle of intelligence developing throughout an endless and unbroken series."

Man can never find his true place in the universe until he recognizes that lower animals are fellow-creatures and, though created inferior in intellect, yet possess all the germs of the intellectual faculties of man. It is somewhat amusing and yet sad to observe the different opinions of scientists on the subject of biology and psychology. The materialist, who traces the origin of sensation and thought from a mere modification of common matter, refers the perceptions and reflections of lower animals to the same principle which produces them in man.

The immaterialist, on the contrary, who conceives that mere matter is incapable, under any modification, of producing sensation and thought, is under the necessity of supplying to every rank of being possessing these powers, the existence of another and of a very different substance combined with it; a substance not subject to the changes and infirmities of matter, and altogether impalpable and incorruptible. Now if sensation and thought can result only from such a substance in man, they can result only from such a substance in lower animals.

The only difficulty arising with the immaterialist, who is influenced by the wrong interpretation of theology, is to know how to dispose of the animal soul on the dissolution of the body. He cannot conceive of the annihilation of an incorruptible, immaterial substance like thought and sensation, according to his own theory, and should admit that, as the faculty of intelligence is discernible in lower animals as well as in man, if this principle is immortal in the one it must be in the other, which is the only proper solution of the question.

CHAPTER VIII

PHYSIOLOGY AND NATURAL THEOLOGY —THE BODY GOVERNED BY IMMATERIAL FORCES

The soul cannot be injured or diseased any more than can electricity, gravity or affinity—It is only the means of communication which can be affected

IT may be of interest, in this connection, to examine some of the most important parts of the bodily structure. Physiology, when properly applied, will assist natural theology to demonstrate that men have souls, and in doing so, it equally proves in every instance that all animals are governed by the same physical and mental laws; and if it can be demonstrated that one animal has a soul, it is conclusive evidence that all have souls.

The nervous system includes the brain, cranial nerves, spinal cord, spinal nerves, and the sympathetic nerve; but the whole system may, for convenience, be placed under two general departments, the first consisting of the brain and its dependencies, and the second of the ganglia and their nervous connections. The first pertains to animal life, conveying impressions calculated to produce sensations, and sending out volitions to its servants, the organs destined to receive them. The second applies to these organs not necessarily under the influence of the will, such as digestion, circulation, respiration, and secretion. Although each nerve is endowed with its own function, yet all the nerves are so bound together that if one suffers all will suffer in some degree.

Those nerves which produce impressions on the brain are called sensory nerves, and no sensation can be excited in any part or organ unless conveyed to the brain, the seat of the soul. For example, the sense of touch resides in the ends of the fingers, and the sense of sight in the eye, yet if the nerve which connects these parts with the brain be divided, no impression is felt, no sensation excited by the organ.

The nerves which convey the orders of the soul to the different organs are called motor nerves. If by the act of the will power the soul sends a portion of nervous influence to a muscle, it immediately contracts, and those parts to which the muscle is attached will move as directed If a man or an ape wishes to bend the arm, he will transmit

through the nerves with which it is supplied, a volition, or act of the soul, to that effect, and the arm
will then bend.

Though the muscles are the instruments of motion, yet such acts are performed through the influence of the soul. If the nerves which supply any
voluntary muscles be divided, the muscles will not
contract.

In partial paralysis, in many forms of tetanus,
such as lock-jaw and cramps, the muscles are not
under control of the soul, yet it is in no way
affected by the lesion.

It has been demonstrated by distinguished physiologists that in one instance or another every part
of the brain has been destroyed or disorganized by
disease or accident, and yet the individuals have
none of them been destitute of the soul and its faculties as long as life continued. The soul cannot
be injured or diseased any more than can electricity,
gravity, or affinity. It is only the means of communication that can be affected.

If the brain, in which some are pleased to lodge
all mental phenomena, has been in one instance or
another destroyed in all its parts without destroying the action of the soul, it is proof positive that

something more than brain matter constitutes animal life. Some animals will continue to live for months after the brain has been destroyed or removed.

It is plainly demonstrated that something which resides in the vital organs governs the body and moves the parts, like a telegraphic system, being under the control of an operator. This life potency feels what is done to it, sees through the eyes, hears through the ears, and is conscious of its own existence. Although the agency of the brain is necessary to the working of the intellectual powers, we are not to conclude that this organ can feel, think, and will of itself; for it is not within the range of possibility to conceive how a material substance can exhibit properties like those of the mind or soul.

There is another fact in this connection which is generally overlooked, and that is, that the soul which presides over the body does not assume the part of a physician, but controls the entire body, as is best, under both normal and abnormal conditions. The soul acts in the same manner towards the body as the providence of God which permits suffering and death as the result of the fall of man.

A parent will exhibit the most tender care and sympathy over his offspring, but cannot relieve suffering nor prevent death. Our Heavenly Father, though He loves all His creatures, and gives them grace to bear their pain, does not agree to change the sentence of suffering and death which is the result of man's disobedience.

The soul, though it presides over and controls the body, is yet powerless to change God's laws. If a person should take some *material* substance, say a large dose of opium, into the body, the brain, from its intimacy with the body, would become affected. If a person should take something *immaterial* into the body, such as love, fear, or grief, the brain would also be affected. Now, if the material stimulus of opium required a material medium through which to act, the immaterial stimulus of love, fear, or grief, must require an immaterial agency, or soul, through which to act. I think this hypothesis is irrefutable, that if a physical stimulus requires a physical agent, as materialists claim, an immaterial stimulus requires an immaterial agent through which the body is acted upon.

Though the brain is the seat of sensation, yet a sensation is referred from an organ to the brain, and from the brain back again to the organ. Pain is, therefore, not felt in any organ, but in the brain, the seat of the soul. If anæsthesia is produced by chloroform, properly administered, as long as the body is under its influence there can be no pain, for the functions of the brain are suspended, but the soul still presides over the body, though its communications are disconnected. The operator is still at headquarters, though the wires are disconnected and there is no communication.

If any portion of the body be removed, the soul presides over what remains as long as there is life. Upon the amputation of a limb, the action of the soul is not found to be diminished, nor any of its faculties lost. When a man loses both arms and both legs, the soul will preside over what remains, and its sphere of action is limited to the remaining part of the body. It cannot make use of that which is not, or which it has not. If the eyes be shut or the ears stopped, it cannot then see or hear, but remove the obstruction, and it instantly assumes its normal condition. This shows that when any sense or faculty becomes impaired or inactive the body loses that instrumentality without affecting the functions of the soul.

My investigation has led me to believe that the soul has its headquarters in the highest forms of matter in each animal. The brain organ whether in high or low species, whether intricate or simple, is used for its office. In the higher species of animals, the soul makes its headquarters in the cerebrum of the brain, and directs the movements of the body as long as life lasts. When one part of the cerebrum is destroyed, the soul occupies the remaining part, and when both hemispheres are removed, as can be done without destroying life in some animals, it establishes its offices in the cerebellum. In a very few animals the cerebellum may be removed without immediate death, and the soul would then make its last move to the medulla oblongata

An animal may be dissected alive, limb after limb, muscle after muscle, nerve after nerve, as some cruel anatomists have done, until but little of the agonizing bloody form is left, and the soul, faithful to its trust, will remain until the merciful angel appears and cries out " it is enough, come up higher." As the destruction of the functions of the ear will not destroy sound, as the destruction of the eye will not destroy light, so the destruction of the body will not destroy the soul. An animal body cannot exist without some existing cause, some force, to give impulse in all vital actions; and as every cause of motion is external to the object moved, all animal life must have some cause which operates and controls the functions of the body outside of the body itself.

I can move my hand upward or downward, faster or slower, or not at all, just as I will. Now if my hand and the power which put it in motion were left to be governed by the law of gravitation or any law governing matter, I would be powerless to make such motions

Thus we perceive there is something within the body which supports it and directs its movements, and which must necessarily be of a different nature from the body.

When a man begins to reflect upon his own nature, he will at once discover that he is a dual being. When he begins to think, he does not know where the thought comes from or in what part of the body it dwells. When he considers his own body, it appears to be something different from the person himself. And when he uses the expression *my body*, or *the body of me*, may it not properly be demanded, who is meant by *me*, or what relation exists between the matter and the soul of the body? It cannot be the body itself that is doing the thinking and talking, for matter cannot do either. If he were all soul or all body, and nothing else, he could not then speak in this manner, because it would be the same as to say *the soul of the soul*, or *the body of the body*, or *the I of me*. The pronoun therefore must stand for something else, of which the body is only a part, or, in other words, there is another part of him which is not body. A lower animal is conscious of its own identity It knows that it is the being which is itself, as it can think, feel, and will, and has the evidence of the existence of both body and soul. Without consciousness, the outward world would have no meaning, and an animal could have no conception of the senses Mind and matter would be one and the same. But we know that matter in itself is inert, senseless, and motionless, as the body would be without the spiritual agent or soul to give it animation, and consciousness of existence.

There is no distinction between man and lower animals in regard to the chemical elements of the body, as they are all composed of the four principal elements, oxygen, hydrogen, carbon, and nitrogen, with the addition of some other elements, such as calcium, phosphorus, potassium, etc. The matter which composes the body of a man is no more complex than that which composes the bodies of the lower animals. Both are subject to the same external and internal forces, vital and physical, and consequently, mind, in some degree, as well as material substance, is found alike in all.

Almost everything in the whole universe is common to both man and the lower animals. They are subject to the general laws of gravitation and force, and are in danger from falls and all impressions of violence. They are subject to disease, injuries, pains, and liable to mental diseases, such as melancholy and insanity. They need nourishment, a proper habitation, protection from wanton abuse, cruelty, or any form of suffering which may possibly be avoided They have a like nervous system which is equally sensitive to all the impressions made upon the body. They are conscious of a liberty to act or not to act, and have a desire for comforts and happiness. They have a social feeling and a desire to love and be loved, and their good and bad dispositions are formed according to their environments.

CHAPTER IX

INSTANCES OF ANIMAL INTELLIGENCE —POWER OF REASONING

If we attribute souls to mankind because of certain intellectual phenomena, we must allow that lower animals have souls for the same reasons—They are governed by a soul principle the same as man

IF we refer certain phenomena in mankind to the possession of souls, we must allow animals to have souls if they produce the same phenomena. Animals perform intellectual operations of various kinds similar to those performed by man ; and, like different races of men, or different men of the same race, they are not all of the same degree of importance.

Animals, like man, have a free will of their own, and their knowledge is acquired by experience We cannot say that they act only automatically. Neither can we ascribe their cunning and comical motions and activities to a being so perfect as Deity. For can Deity be supposed to be taught to swear and talk obscenely in a parrot, or to chatter the absurd and irreverent language of a magpie ?

Can you fancy that He gives the body of an animal this or that motion, or places it in this or that particular attitude at the sound of a curse, the crack of a whip, or from arbitrary signs of human actions?

The Bible plainly attributes the principle of distinct knowledge and free-will to lower animals in the passage which says, "For the stork in the heavens knoweth her appointed times, and the turtle and the crane and the swallow know the times of their coming, but My people do not understand the judgments of their God." It is evident by this that an animal acts upon an intelligent principle of its own; for if its motions were the effect of infinite intelligence, the inspired writer was very wrong in introducing it as an instance of regularity to shame man's follies and awaken him to a sense of his duty or the call of his God. Hence animals are to be considered as creatures that move and act of themselves, or as having souls like man by which they are informed and directed. The memory of animals, their power of comparing, distinguishing, and reasoning, and, above all, their sense, which necessarily infers a sentient principle, are additional confirmations of this truth never to be shaken. They move in consequence of sensations received, are susceptible of durable affection, can acquire by experience a knowledge of things by which they are governed, and have a foresight of consequences When under the control of superiors, they feel their subordination, know that the being who punishes them may refrain from so doing, if he will, and when sensible of having done wrong, or beholding their superior angry, will assume a suppliant and depreciatory action, and will make an effort to apologize and seek forgiveness. They are susceptible of emulation, jealousy, love, fear, and other faculties possessed by mankind.

They readily show gratitude for kind treatment, and become so attached to a friend that they will attempt to defend him from an enemy at the sacrifice of their own lives. They have rushed through flames of fire to warn their friends of approaching danger. Dogs have saved the lives of many children by plunging into streams of water and dragging them out. They go into distant mountains amidst the most severe snow-storms, and hunt and rescue the lost and perishing.

They will risk their lives to defend their young, and have often been known to feed and care for a helpless companion. Every species has a language peculiar to itself, by means of which all the individuals that compose it are able to converse with each other, to impart their love, their pains, their fears, and their desires. They, like man, when driven to extreme mental and physical suffering, as a last resort, will deliberately commit suicide. Many sad instances are on record of domestic animals, forsaken or abused in such a cruel manner that they have voluntarily drowned or starved themselves to death.

If it were necessary I could give numerous well-authenticated illustrations to prove each of the mental actions I have attributed to animals, but as most persons have seen and read a sufficient number to be convinced that the statements are correct, it would be a useless undertaking. I have heard related by truthful persons so many marvelous acts of the lower animals, and have seen so many myself, that I am ready to believe almost anything I hear or read on the subject. They build houses and provide homes, and live in separate families. They are capable of education, and a few species learn to articulate the language of man. They converse with each other in their own language by articulating sounds which they vary into different tones and manner of expression, and, like man, have a silent way of communicating their ideas by gestures, looks, and signs. They had a language given them long before man was created, and the chief addition which has been made to it is the sound-signs used by man. Some animals are capable of uttering a great number of specific sounds, and yet we call them dumb simply because we do not understand their language. Mocking-birds, starlings, ravens, parrots, magpies, and some other species, learn to talk, sing, whistle, and imitate the various sounds they hear. They are taught to converse in different languages, and answer in the same language in which they are addressed. Dogs and monkeys may be taught to use as many specific sounds and signs for specific things as some of the lowest types of man, which shows that they are capable of a progressive education. Many animals have the power of reasoning wonderfully developed. An elephant will break off a branch of a tree, grasp it in his trunk and drive off the flies. He will blow beyond an object he cannot reach, and drive it towards him. When sick, he will go alone to a surgeon for treatment.

Dogs, squirrels, and many other animals will hide away food for future use, and thus acquire and hold property. Birds repair broken limbs with as much skill as a human surgeon. When the dear little creatures have their wings and legs splintered and broken by the cruel sportsman, they form, around the fracture, a splint made of feathers plucked from their bodies, mixed with mud or coagulated blood, which resembles a plaster cast, such as surgeons use.

A horse, when losing a shoe or becoming lame in the foot, will go to a blacksmith shop where he has been shod, in order to receive help.

A dog, when wounded, will go to a friend for assistance, and if he receives it, will return every day until he is cured. If he chances to find another lame dog, he will take him to the same person for help.

Thus animals show a power of choice and of determination, guided by a perception of the nature of the object to be obtained, and the means to be employed, exhibiting a great degree of the reasoning faculties They are sensitive to kindness or abuse, and are melancholy or happy according to their environments.

When we observe the sagacity of a dog, a monkey,

an elephant, a horse, or any other intelligent ani
mal, and the great variety of ways in which it
will display an intelligent adaptation of means
to ends, laying aside what is usually called instinct,
we must conclude that the faculties of man and
animals are unlike only in degree   Animals are
taught by example, by the imitation and instructions of others of the same species, and also by
different species, to perform various acts of intelligence, and these acts do not differ from man's so
far as the brain action is concerned

Animals are progressive in the manner of receiving
their education in all actions, the same as man. Take
a puppy, for instance, and observe his gradual development, and the different mental stages of action,
and you will notice he adds new thoughts and actions,
and leaves many features of his early life behind when
he grows older, just as we see in the gradual development of a child.   Take a young canary bird, and
you will observe that its first notes are imperfect,
like a child learning to talk, but by a constant
effort it will become proficient.   At first young
animals are slow and awkward, move imperfectly,
do things incorrectly, but as they grow older, they
improve, and move and act more correctly.   In many

instances they are observed to change their usual modes of operation, to better attain particular ends, and in many things are capable of a proficiency that is amazing. Within the last half century, wild as well as domestic animals have been taught to do many wonderful things hitherto considered impossible. It has been stated by the best authority that lower animals, as well as man, are making great advancement in intellectual development, and as John Wesley says, "What if it should please the all-wise, the all-gracious Creator to raise them higher in the scale of beings, and when He makes us equal to angels, to make them what we are now?" But before passing from this subject it would be well to call attention to the fact that there is often great abuse in teaching animals to do unnatural and dangerous things. They should not be required to perform acts which cannot be taught by kind and gentle means. Any other method is cruel and unwarrantable, and should be prohibited by law.

The monkey so plainly imitates man, that he is sometimes classed as a lower type of the same species. This cunning animal, being so extremely imitative, will mimic almost every gesture or act he sees man do, and has such a powerful memory that he will repeat the tricks many years afterwards. He has been taught to sit at the table, and eat with knife, fork, and spoon. He will put sugar in tea, stir it up, pour it into a saucer, and drink and eat with as much ease and decorum as a human being. He will wear clothing, and perform many acts of useful labor, such as cleaning boots, brushing clothes, churning, and acting in the capacity of waiter. Under a systematic education, the ape, orang-outang, and chimpanzee have been taught to perform many wonderful things. In their native home, they live in families, construct huts, and defend themselves against their enemies by the use of clubs, stones, and other missiles; and in mental and physical actions, differ but little from the lower type of mankind.

As we observe the several faculties and traits of character, which belong alike to man and animals, we recognize that some knowledge of things is born with them and some acquired by a degree of education. They are no sooner born than they seek and greedily embrace remedies to supply hunger and all bodily wants. A lamb or a babe without any instructions will seek the proper nourishment from its mother.

A young bird will open its mouth and cry for food upon the approach of its parents. A chicken, as soon as it is out of the shell, will pick up grains of wheat, hide itself under the wings of the hen, and fly from the approach of danger. Cattle feeding in the pasture are more skilful than man in discriminating between herbs or plants, for they easily discern what kinds are good for food, what for medicine, and what are to be shunned as poison.

This important fact has often been mentioned by ancient writers. Pliny said that it was a shame that all animals knew what was healthful for themselves except man. They perform not only what may be termed simple actions caused by necessity, but complex actions where choice can come only from reason. They will travel a great distance to find a cool place in the shade; will return to their former homes when transported for hundreds of miles away; and will remember their friends after many years' absence. Birds, by reason of spring-time, choose a companion, enter into wedlock by a solemn manner of espousal, and are true to death. They select a fit place for building their nest or habitation, and make it most artistic and beautiful, beyond the skill of a human architect. They lay eggs and, sitting on them by turns to keep them warm, bring forth young ones, and jointly and carefully nourish these until they are able to take care of themselves.

If a horse is feeding, and the ground becomes bare, he calls to mind another place, though it be miles away, where he knows food is more plentiful, and at once goes to that spot. He will raise and lower a pump handle in order to get a drink of water, and will ring a bell for his meals.

A dog knows a man at a great distance, and recognizes in him either a friend or an enemy. If a friend, he runs to meet him, and shows by his actions that he loves him; but if an enemy, he flies at him with anger, or goes away from him in disgust. In considering, in lower animals, the instances of fidelity, of sagacity, of cunning, of attachment, of gratitude, and of the way they change their minds to accomplish different purposes, as well as the difference between old and young in point of experience and usefulness, we cannot fail to perceive a degree of reason which is in many respects superior to that of some of the lowest types of men.

We find the faculty of reason in lower animals so well developed, and each individual act so diversified and adapted to times, places, and circumstances, and means to ends, that if man is beholden to reason for his power of adaptation, we must also admit that lower animals are likewise possessed of a great degree of rationality.

A dog will recognize its master, but it must be an effort of memory which enables it to seek him when lost, to perform the tricks it has been taught, or the services it is called upon to render. There must be memory or there would be no recognition.

We are told that a horse, after being absent for eleven years, when he returned to his former home, remembered his owner, his stall, the way through the fields to the brook for water, the spots where he used to find the best grass, and seemed to recognize all the unchanged surroundings.

A dog returned to his former home after an absence of eight years, and remembered his former owner and all the surroundings. An elephant was known to remember a former keeper it had not seen for seventeen years, and at the first request, readily performed some tricks taught by him that it had not performed since that time.

A poor man in Edinburgh, Scotland, by the name of Grey, owned a bright little dog named Bobby;

and he and his dog were wonderfully attached to each other. Mr. Grey finally died, and poor little Bobby fully realized the sad loss of his best friend. He followed his master to the grave and was the saddest mourner in the procession.

He refused to leave, and the sexton found him lying on the grave next morning. As it was against the rules to allow dogs in the cemetery, he was put out, but he found his way back ; and for several mornings in succession he was found lying on his master's grave. James Brown, the old sexton of the cemetery, was a very kind man and took pity on poor little heart-broken Bobby, and not only allowed him to remain on the grave, but gave him his regular meals for some time, until a kind-hearted restaurant keeper took the matter in charge, and the dog was fed and properly taken care of until he died at the ripe age of twelve years. During many years, though he had many warm friends, and the offer of luxurious homes (which he declined), every night, and through all kinds of weather, he slept on his master's grave The grave of that poor man has long since been obscured by time, and nothing marks the spot. Not so the memory of the faithful dog; a beautiful monument was erected by Baroness Burdett Coutts, to commemorate poor little Bobby's undying affection for his master. Such mental action as was manifested by Bobby cannot possibly be of a material nature, but belongs to the highest attributes of the soul

The horse does not forget the road he has once traversed, though years may have intervened. Dogs, elephants, monkeys, and other animals, recognize persons from whom they have received kindness, after a long separation. Some have been known to treasure up the recollections of wrongs, and have watched for opportunities for revenge many years after the abuse.

It is by such phenomena of the animal soul that we recognize its power of perception. The different kinds of perceptions are as numerous as the different channels through which they are received, and they are durable in proportion to the exciting cause. These impressions, as they are retained, become ideas. The mind has the power of suffering such ideas to remain latent or unobserved, and of calling them into observation at its option ; and it is the active exercise of this power that constitutes thought. Reason is founded in the consciousness of thoughts by which actions are governed, and is the internal evidence of conscious thoughts and the power to arrive at a conclusion. To be governed by reason or abstract ideas is a general law imposed by the Creator upon all animals. An orang-outang, in Paris, when left alone, tried to escape; and as he could not reach the lock of his door, he carried a stool to the spot, and mounting upon it, took his master's keys and tried each one until finding the right one, he unlocked the door as he had seen his master do, and walked out. Reason only could have prompted this act, as it would require a combination of ideas to perform it.

It is plain that reason is of a commanding nature. It enjoins this, condemns that, and approves or disapproves things as may be best suited to the notion of the animal.

A dog will grieve to death over the memory of a lost master, as was the case with the dog of Emile Zola, the noted French author. While he was an exile, his faithful and loving dog, after searching everywhere for several days and failing to find his devoted master, died of a broken heart. Zola says: "It seemed to me as if my departure had killed him, and I wept like a child. Even now it is impossible for me to think of him without being moved to tears. When I returned, a corner of the house seemed empty Of all my sacrifices, the death of my dog in my absence has been one of the hardest. This sort of thing is ridiculous, I know; and if I tell it it is because I am sure to find in you a tender heart for animals, and one who will not laugh too much."

One of my neighbors had a bright and beautiful Maltese cat which seemed to be the idol of the family. The lady of the house would caress it and talk to it like a child, and it seemed to have formed an unusual attachment for her; but they decided to move to California, and before doing so, gave the cat to another family who succeeded them in the same building. Poor pussy soon recognized the absence of its mistress, and would go from room to room in search of her, uttering a low, pitiful, calling noise. Although the new occupants of the house were kind and gentle, and did all they could to reconcile the cat, the poor little animal pined away, and died of grief.

A creature possessing such a determining and governing power, is certainly a creature formed to be governed by that power. It seems to

be as much designed by nature, or rather the
Author of nature, that animals should use their
reason, and be guided by it, as that the pilot,
in the design of the ship-wright, should direct
the vessel by the use of the rudder he has fitted
to it.

It is rare nowadays to find a man so heartless and
silly as to believe the absurd doctrine of Descartes
and Malebranche, that the lower animals are devoid of conscious feeling. It seems impossible for
any intelligent person to think that a log of wood
and a sensitive animal are alike as to sensibility;
that an animal has no more feeling under the
blows of a whip or the cut of a knife, than the log
has under the strokes of a carpenter's ax Why
is it that the one cries out with pain and the
other remains silent ? Is it not evident therefore
that the animal is sensible of pain, and the log
of wood has no such perception ? The expression
of pain is more marked than that of joy in the
features of lower animals, and extends even to
the shedding of tears in almost all animals when
undergoing intense agony. The physical signs of
pain consist of changes in circulation and temper-
ature, quickened respiration, dilation of the iris,

and distorted countenance, all of which are visible in lower animals as well as in man.

Man and the lower animals are equally supplied with sensory nerves and are equally subject to pain. It is not consistent with the nature of the laws of the Creator that He should make a nerve for man which is capable of sensibility, and one just like it in appearance, for lower animals, which is incapable of feeling.

No physiologist has yet been able to make such a distinction. How necessary, then, that animals should be treated as sensitive beings, and not as automata. That they have reason controlled by the will is as well demonstrated as it is that man has that faculty

It is by reason and will power that migratory birds are capable of steering, with the precision of a compass, from one climate or country to another; and which if possessed by man, might render useless the compass for a like purpose.

Carrier-pigeons have been taken hundreds of miles away, and when let loose, have returned to their homes in the most direct line. Dogs, cats, horses, and other animals, will also return to their homes from a great distance. Thus we are compelled to confess that animals are endowed with discriminating powers totally unknown to or attainable by man.

Man cannot be regarded as distinguished from other animals either by acuteness of sensibility or by muscular power. His swiftness in running and agility in leaping are not of a high order. That portion of the nervous system distributed to the organs of sense, is less developed in man than it is in most animals. He is surpassed by many creatures in acuteness of sight, sound, and scent.

The power of birds to navigate the air is a favor shown them which does not belong to man That a body so much heavier than air should overcome the force of gravity, and soar far above the earth, and, by overcoming the resistance of the atmosphere, go directly against the current of wind, is wonderful to contemplate.

While the intellectual faculties of man are superior to those of animals, that faculty of the soul called instinct is far stronger in animals.

CHAPTER X

INSTINCT IS IMMORTAL —DIFFERENCE BETWEEN EDUCATED AND UNEDUCATED ANIMALS

Various faculties of the soul—All common to man and lower animals—Instinct the highest attribute of the soul—It is knowledge direct from God.

BEFORE proceeding further with this subject it will be best to explain what is meant by the word *instinct*, as it is wrongfully used by most theologians. It is a faculty of the soul, and is characterized by unconscious, spontaneous action as determined by the creatures' wants and necessities. The word is not found in the Bible, and, like many other words used by the Church, its effect is to lower intelligent acts emanating from the despised animal creation.

The nature of mind and instinct involves the nature of God, and cannot be divided by some unknown and uncertain mystical line. Instinct is not only an attribute of the soul, but the very highest faculty that it possesses. The Creator deals more directly with the creature under the law governing instinct than any known law in the great cosmos.

Instinct is the highest attribute God possesses, and a man who would deny that it is immortal, could with the same consistency, deny that the omniscience, omnipotence, or any other attribute of God, is immortal. Instinct is so closely interwoven with all the phenomena we see and know around us, that if it is not an immortal attribute of God, we know of nothing that is. It is knowledge from God, directly imparted to animals, not once, but continually; and we do not know where it begins nor where it ends.

It is claimed by theology that the innate idea of immortality is instinctive in man, as it exists in some rude form or other even where individuals and nations have never heard of it through man.

Now as animals are endowed with instinct superior to man, they may have an instinctive idea revealed to them that they too are immortal. Who knows that they have not? The fact that a man desires immortality gives him no better assurance of it than if he did not desire it, provided there is no provision for him. Every man desires comforts and happiness here on earth, and he would naturally desire that condition continued throughout all eternity.

Animals desire comforts and happiness here on earth. That they have no instinct which leads them to desire a continuance of these blessings in another world is an assumption that no man has ever proven or has any moral right to make.

An idiot, a child, or a heathen could not have a desire for immortality unless it were instinctive. The intelligence of man and of lower animals is in proportion to the amount and quality of instinctive knowledge. All animals are, in some degree, rational beings; and the superiority of man is due, not to his bodily formation, but to the great variety of instincts which emanate from divine wisdom.

Instinct includes more of the faculties of man than is generally admitted. Take the lowest races of man, and you will observe that almost all of their mental actions are instinctive, from the fact that their wants are analogous to the wants of the lower animals, but this does not imply that they are any less entitled to a soul than some great philosopher.

It is common to say, when an animal performs some important mental action, it is instinct; but if a man performs the same thing it is called reason. Most of the phenomena of life are made up of what is common to man and the lower animals, and if it is instinct in one it is in all.   It is common to eat when hungry; to rest when tired; to sleep when sleepy; to love or hate; to fear pain or death; to recognize a friend or an enemy; and to seek comfort and happiness.

The highest aim of man and the lower animals is the possession or pursuit of bodily wants.   Man, besides being man, is also an animal, and is governed by the same physical and mental laws; and freewill no more belongs to him than to other animals. The only difference is that the mind of animals is acted upon by fewer and simpler motives.   Animals are free to go in any direction; free to eat, drink, walk, run, lie down, quarrel, fight, go astray, trespass on the rights of others, and follow out the bent of their minds, and, like man, free to act any part of life which their organizations may permit them to do   If I say to my dog, "Give me your paw," and hold out my hand, it will cheerfully do so.   If I say to a little child, "Give me your hand," it will comply with my request. I say to a horse, "Lie down," and to a boy, "Lie down," they will both obey my command. I say to a dog, "Bring me my hat," and to a boy, "Bring me my cane," and they will both do as directed. The mental action and free-will is reason in one as well as the other. At some time in their lives each one had to be taught the relation between the articulate sounds of my voice, and each had to reason from the different sounds I uttered which act I wished performed. A child will look up into my face and say, "Please open the door," being unable to do so itself. My cat will go to the door, pat it with its paw, and look trustfully up into my face and say, "Please open the door." I understand one just as well as the other, though they do not articulate the same kind of sounds. Both go on the principle of reasoning from cause to effect. They ask me to open the door, as they know by that act, they can walk outside through the open space and be at liberty to go where they choose.

If this vital energy is the product of the soul in the one instance it is in all. In infancy, theology says, that the child is governed by instinct, but as it grows older, that form of instinct which was necessary for its existence disappears. Now if an infant has a soul, according to theology, while under the government of instinct, it is certainly the vital cause of all its actions. So that instinct is the immortal part of the child.

In the lowest types of the human race, instinct forms the human constitution, and there are instances where there are no traces of any faculty above instinct. If such types of mankind have souls, and are governed by only one form of vital energy, it is certainly soul energy.

The same argument may be used in the case of an idiot or lower animals We perceive the diversified operations of the soul and call this energy by different names according to different manifestations. When inferring truth from truth, it is called understanding; when tracing a cause to an effect, it is reasoning; when contemplating the future, imagination; when reviewing the past, memory; when choosing or refusing, will; and when spontaneous, instinct.

As they all refer to the phenomena of vital action, and there is but one soul to each being, it must be true that the soul has many faculties, or else it has nothing to do in controlling the body.

When observing the faculty of *love*, which is the highest attribute of the soul, and the strongest tie that binds together all living creatures, we are bound to acknowledge that it is manifested in a greater degree in lower animals than in man.

Christ says, "Greater love hath no man than this, that a man lay down his life for his friends" That lower animals, especially dogs, have repeatedly sacrificed their lives for their friends, no one will pretend to deny.

The famous St. Bernard dog, Barry, of Switzerland, in a period of ten years, at the risk of his own life, saved forty-one lives. One of his most creditable achievements was when he found a child of ten years buried in the snow succumbing to the fatal slumber which precedes death. The noble dog first warmed the child with his breath, and licked it till it woke. Then by lying on his side close to the child, he gave it an obvious invitation to get upon his back, which the child did, and Barry carried it safely home. Barry went out during one dismal, cold snow-storm into the high, bleak Alpine mountains, and after making a long journey finally found a man in a snow bank. Barry was always delighted to know he could be the means of saving one more life. He commenced to bark for assistance, and to tug and coax the half-frozen man, in order to awake him and receive any message the man might be able to send in for help; but the man was unfortunately ignorant of the dog's proffered kindness, and beat poor Barry over the head until he was dead; and thus Barry gave his life, as many have done, a sacrifice to man's blind and hasty judgment. The kind people of Switzerland have recently erected a large and beautiful monument to the memory of poor faithful Barry; and I here declare, that there is not another monument on earth I would prefer to have assisted in building.

A short time ago, I read this incident in an eastern paper. A little girl was playing on a wharf when she fell into the water, and was washed out some distance from the shore. Her faithful dog plunged after her, and by great and prolonged effort brought the child near enough to be lifted out by some person who had rushed to the rescue; but the poor dog was so exhausted that he could not accept assistance, and sank beneath the waves to rise no more.

The New York *Times* gives an account of a fire

in a large barn and carriage house. A dog kept in the barn ran up-stairs and aroused the coachman who had scarcely time to escape through the window. The dog did not attempt to follow, but being encouraged by his success in saving his master, returned to the lower floor, and made a great, though pitiful effort to save the horses, but without success, and all perished together.

A farmer of Winnamac, Indiana, was moving his family into an adjoining county; and on starting, placed the seven-months-old babe in the care of its brother, who, getting tired of carrying it, laid it in a basket beside a bush, near a steep bluff, and followed on without it. On arriving at the new farm the grief-stricken mother, missing the baby, was frantic; and started back for the spot where the babe had been left. In a short time she met their faithful dog " Ned " with the babe. He had discovered it, and was lugging it safely along. As soon as the happy mother received her child, poor Ned lay down and died from exhaustion. The affection of the dog for the child was greater than that of the child's brother. Such self-sacrifice can only be compared to the rarest and noblest acts of man. Such noble animals take the risk, with the knowledge of the danger and the dread of the exposure. The strange feeling of affection enables them to overcome the fear of risks, even of death itself, in order to save the lives of friends. And they show their consciousness of having performed such moral acts by their manifestation of joy for any approbation bestowed on them. They not only give themselves as a sacrifice, but make intercession for the welfare and protection of others.

My kinsman, Gen. S. B. Buckner, on one occasion, was so deeply impressed by the actions of a dog that he promptly relieved the distress of a heart-broken woman

The Louisville *Courier-Journal* tells the beautiful and touching story in the following language: "That was a fine passage between the Executive of Kentucky and the wife of the condemned man, who went to Frankfort last Friday to ask for a pardon. She had presented her papers and sat breathless whilst the arbiter of her fate perused them. As she waited, a mastiff, the playmate of the Governor's little son, an animal not given to strangers, uncoiled himself from the rug where he had been lying, and came up in that friendly way which only dogs know how to affect with perfect

sincerity. Seeing suspense and pain in the agitated
features of the poor woman, he put his paws gently
upon her knees and began to lick her hands. The
Governor finished the papers and the petitioner
was about to speak, when the grim old soldier said,
'It is not necessary, madam, the dog has spoken
for you,' and straightway signed the document
which was to release a dying man from prison and
enable him to go to his grave from his own home.
One touch of nature makes the whole world kin,
and it is hard to say which moves us the more, the
spectacle of that brave gentleman and soldier,
whom it was a delight and pride to hail as our
chief magistrate, stirred to the depth by the silent
eloquence of a dog, or the thought of that noble
brute, inspired by we know not what, to become an
irresistible pleader for mercy before the highest
court. The incident makes a seasonable text. Indeed, there was as much of truth as sarcasm in the
observation of the cynic, who declared that the
more he saw of men the better he thought of dogs.

" The love of a dog has nothing sordid nor treach-
erous about it. The poor beast knows not how to
dissemble. Governor Buckner knew his son's dog
believed in him And, when he saw the animal

make common cause with the grief-stricken woman,
he felt that, if he followed the lead of that dog's pity
and love he could make no mistake. And he did
not; and then and there the angel that writes in a
book drew a great white mark for that Governor
and that dog "

But no person is competent to judge of the nature of any species of animal until he has had one
of that kind as a pet, and has become intimately acquainted with it by a long and fond association,
and subjected it to a kind and gentle education.
The difference between the educated and un-
educated lower animals is as great as that between
the savage and civilized man. We must study the
nature of lower animals, and endeavor to think as
they think, feel as they feel, and in a sense, place
ourselves in their position We must regard them
as little children with limited intellects willing to
do our bidding if they can comprehend it. Different families become attached to different animals. One family will make a pet of their dog
and neglect their cat, another will make a pet of
their cat and neglect their dog, but we must learn
all the particular traits of an animal to know its
intelligent and loving disposition.

When I gaze into the happy and loving face of an intelligent animal and observe the eyes sparkling with animated life, hope, and trust, I become absorbed in contemplation of a profound mystery I see plainly shining through the eyes, which act as windows of heaven, an immortal soul in the background. A dog will sit and gaze into a man's face for hours as if he were trying to understand the nature of his superior.

Man, in like manner, will gaze into the ethereal sky trying to understand something of the mysterious nature of God. We have often noticed a dog, on a clear beautiful night, when all Nature seemed asleep, sit for hours and gaze into the starry heavens and utter a pathetic, doleful cry. What it means has never been satisfactorily explained, but that it is some instinctive devotion is the most reasonable conclusion. Savages who never heard of the Bible have the same habit.

Theology offers no other reason for denying souls to lower animals than the simple fact that they are not of the same species as man. The fact that others do not belong to the same species or race has been man's excuse for cruelty throughout his history. Slavery was once considered legitimate by all civilized nations, as the slaves were of a different and subordinate race to their masters. The robbery and murder of foreigners are considered legitimate to-day by some countries, and the savage who can boast of the most scalps of other tribes or races is the greatest hero Though men may be cannibals and though they may be ignorant and cruel, live in caves and holes in the ground, go naked, and subsist on herbs, roots, snakes, and lizards, and occasionally roast a fat missionary, yet they are never denied the possession of souls; while innocent, helpless animals are conceived of as being without this God-given endowment. How narrow and contracted such a system of theology to discriminate thus against any of God's creatures.

History is a very important factor in holding mankind responsible for any great wrong committed individually or collectively. Less than a century ago a book was published, in this country, based upon the hypothesis that the African race did not have souls, and according to the history of the case, a large number of good people were persuaded to believe in its arguments. The Mahom-

medans, at the present time, deny the right of
woman to a soul equal to man.

We read in Grecian history of "seven wise men"
who met at regular intervals and formulated
systems of philosophy, and then sent them forth
into the world for people to accept as indisputable.
A similar historical analogy would be that of a few
learned theologians getting together and decreeing
that no one should have souls but themselves or
their special race

We hope the day is not far distant when
theology will become more Christlike, and include
under the atonement the whole creation that
groaneth and travaileth in-pain and sorrow.

One of the arguments of theology to prove the
immortality of man, is the assertion of the fact
that the body is undergoing constant changes and
that yet the identity remains the same. We are
told by physiologists that every element of the
body changes once in from three to seven years.
And yet the body is regarded as one and the same
throughout such changes. Neither mind nor disposition is changed by this molecular change of the
body.

The same man of to-day has not an individual

particle belonging to him of that which constituted his corporal frame a few years ago, yet he knows that the soul which thinks within him, notwithstanding all these changes, is the same; and he is the same person, who many years ago, played in such a field, went to such a school, and performed such acts common to life

Now if this argument adds anything to the proof of the immortality of the soul of man, inasmuch as all other animal bodies undergo the same kind of changes and retain their identity, there is a strong presumption that they too have immortal souls.

Another argument often used to indicate the immortality of man is that of showing how each individual differs from all others. It is claimed that no two persons are alike in looks, walk, voice, or actions, and that the mental faculties are entirely peculiar to each person; and yet this is equally true as applied to animals. Although a flock of sheep, a herd of cattle, or a number of fowls, or a corral of horses may look alike, yet each one can be readily recognized by intimate acquaintance.

The fact that man possesses a faculty for enjoying happiness and that all do not receive an equal share of it in this life, has been used as an argument for a future life in order to equalize conditions.

I am perfectly willing to admit the reasonableness of the argument, but at the same time must urge the claims of lower animals by the same logic. Notwithstanding the subordinate condition of lower animals, enjoyment is the proper attendant of their existence, and we perceive everywhere, when it is within their power to attain, symptoms of enjoyment and happiness. Their whole being is a system of needs, the supply of which is a gratification, and of faculties, the exercise of which is pleasurable.

They more extensively enjoy the happiness which is limited to their sphere than man in his sphere, as their mental and bodily functions are less liable to interfere with their enjoyment. To form so vast a range of beings, and to make beings everywhere capable of happiness is a conclusive argument that the destiny of all must be the same. The faculties of the various species differ, the same as the different races of man; but the happiness of each depends on the harmony there may be between its particular faculties and its particular environments. If their bodily wants are supplied, and they have pleasant and comfortable surroundings, they rest in a peaceful and passive manner.

Place a sheep, cow, or horse in a green pasture supplied with shade and water and it will fully enjoy the harmony of relations.

In the highest type of man, owing to his superior organization, he craves more bodily comforts, but the harmony of the surroundings must be in accordance with the capacity of the intellect, for there are many types of the human race that do not reach higher than animal wants, and when accustomed to their condition, are just as happy. The same is true of all animals; there is a general adaptation to the mental and physical constitution for every species and condition of life. Their social qualities are of a high degree, and afford them mutual love and enjoyment.

Their playful nature is a positive evidence of their capacity for happiness. Horses gallop hither and thither, snort, paw the air, advance towards their master, stop suddenly, and again dash off as if to play a joke.

Dogs when kindly treated and among their friends are the happiest creatures in the world, not excepting man; but when abused and forsaken are the most wretched. They are as much delighted with play as a child, and seem to enjoy the company of man more than their own species.

Cats, when properly cared for and trained, are the most affectionate creatures on earth, and yet they are the most abused. They will play hide-and-seek, gambol and frolic when young, and if kindly treated will retain the same disposition until they arrive at a good old age.

Birds will chase each other about in play, and chatter with delight as they go from branch to branch.

We see only a very small part of the works and ways of God in animal creation, as they are infinite in extent; and yet we see enough to inspire us with the confidence that " His tender mercies are over all His works," and extend to all His creatures.

A sparrow falleth not to the ground without His care, and the very hairs of the head of a man are numbered; " how excellent is Thy loving-kindness, O God, Thou preserver of man and beast." If His tender mercies are over all, would He give eternal life to one and eternal annihilation to another ?

CHAPTER XI

ANATOMICAL ANALOGY OF ANIMALS —COMPARATIVE PSYCHOLOGY

A close similarity of animals—A corresponding structure and gradation from one species to another—Lower animals possess every incipient principle of man—This uniformity of design furnishes proof of the unity and wisdom of the Creator

I HAVE been speaking of the intellectual powers of lower animals in order to show that they possess minds, or souls, analogous to man.

Let us now briefly consider the analogy of man and lower animals from an anatomical standpoint. We are taught by comparative anatomy that there is a close similarity in the bodily structure of all animals, and that each species possesses many things common to all.

When we consider the various organs of animals separately and trace them through the same class, we find they exist in a regular and uniform manner, and often observe a part or vestige of a part of no use, left, it seems, by the all-wise Creator, in order that the general law of unity might not be transgressed. One organ is at its highest state of perfection in one species of animals and another organ is the most perfect in a different species, so that if the species are to be arranged after each particular organ, there must be as many scales formed, as there are regulating organs assumed. You cannot construct a general scale of perfection which will apply to all animals.

No two species sufficiently resemble each other to form a proper band of connection, and yet there is a uniformity of structure in all, and only five distinct plans upon which the animal structure is classified by zoölogists. Take the monkey which is of the mammalia class, and most nearly related to man, and the anatomical arrangements are the same, bone for bone, and muscle for muscle, and yet you can take the sternum, ribs, legs, arms, and hands of a lizard, and they too correspond to that of man. The limbs of all the vertebrate animals are of the same plan, however various they may appear. In the hind leg of a horse, for example, the angle called the hock is the same part which in man forms the heel, and the horse, and many other quadrupeds, walk upon what answer to the toes of a human being. In many animals the fore part of the extremities is shrunk up in the hoof, as the tail or coccyx of man is shrunk up and hidden by bones and flesh. The membrane of the bat called wings is formed chiefly upon bones answering precisely to those of the human hand. In the paddles of a whale, the flippers of the seal and other animals of the like species we see the same design.

If you take the skeleton of a man; incline the bones of the pelvis; shorten those of the thighs, legs, and arms; join the phalanges of the fingers and toes; lengthen the jaws by shortening the frontal bones; and lastly extend the spine of the back, this skeleton would no longer represent that of a man, but would resemble the skeleton of a horse.

By lengthening the back bone and the jaws, the number of the vertebra, ribs and teeth, would be increased, and it is only by the number of these bones and by the prolongation, contraction, and junction of others that the skeleton of a horse differs from that of a man. The ribs which are essential to the figure of lower animals are found equally in man, in quadrupeds, in birds, in fishes, and even in the turtle.

The foot of the horse, so apparently different

from the hand of man, is composed of similar bones, and at the extremity of each finger, we have the same small bones resembling the hand, which are bound up in the hoof of that animal.

If the skeleton of quadrupeds, from the ape to the mouse, be lifted up and placed by the side of man there will be observed a surprising uniformity of structure in the whole group. This uniformity is so constant, and the gradations from one species to another are so perfect that to discover the marks of difference requires careful discrimination. There is a corresponding structure on a common plan for all animals. The hand of man, the paw of the dog, the fin of the whale, the wing of the bird, the foot of the horse, and the wing of the bat are not alike in outward appearance, and are used for a different purpose, yet they have an equal number of bones differently lengthened and arranged for the different purposes for which they were intended. And as the bones of man are analogous to the bones of lower animals, so are the muscles, nerves, blood-vessels, viscera, and entire structure of the body. Man walks on two legs, and so do all feathered animals as well as some other species such as the gorilla, orang-outang, kangaroo, etc.

In comparative psychology we are met with still more interesting phenomena.

The intelligence of lower animals is a profound mystery to us. We do not know what they think, nor the extent of their thoughts, but I am positive they have much more intelligence than is usually attributed to them, and that the germ of every human faculty exists in some form and in some species of animals. As one man does not possess all the faculties which the mind is capable of possessing, so it is with the faculty of any one of the lower animals, but in the aggregate they possess every incipient principle of every known faculty in man It is a matter of fact that the size of the brain does not determine the power of the intellect, neither in man nor in lower animals. The whale, elephant, and many other animals have larger brains than man. And in the proportion of brain weight to body weight there are many lower animals which have larger brains in proportion to the weight of the body than man. The proportions of man represent one-fiftieth, while he is surpassed by some species of ape which vary from one-twenty-eighth to one-thirteenth, and some species of bird which range from one-twenty-seventh to one-twelfth.

When man attempts to build up some strong line of difference between himself and some particular lower animal, he will find that that difference is supplied in some other species. Thus the Creator has given us to understand we must acknowledge a kinship to all animals. There is a relationship, by descent, between all species of the animal kingdom, as each species has descended from its own progenitor, and all progenitors have one common Parent or Creator. This is the Bible theory of evolution, and the one which most all naturalists admit, though variously modified by some.

While the Supreme Being has employed one general plan, He at the same time diversified it in every possible manner, so that we must admire equally the magnificence of the execution and the harmony and simplicity of creation. Purpose, intention, and design everywhere strike the most careless and the most stupid thinker. The Creator does nothing in vain, and acts by the simplest methods and chooses the most proper means to every end. As our knowledge of nature enlarges we gradually learn to combine the presumptions arising from analogy, with other general principles which are corrected and improved by such knowledge.

But lest I should be misunderstood I reluctantly advert to a subject I would much prefer not to introduce. Some modern scientists have assumed the hypothesis that the ancestors of the human race originally sprung from the mammalia next highest to man. This theory has been advocated by several learned naturalists of Europe, but Charles Darwin is the modern champion of the theory that man and lower animals descended from " only four or five progenitors "

While I admire Darwin's great mental labors and his profound researches into the dark and hidden mysteries of nature, yet there is no doubt his theory has been a great hindrance to the cause of humanity, and has worked a great hardship to suffering animal life. It has had a tendency to cause some Christians to draw a wider distinction between themselves and the lower animals. They do not desire to be considered on Darwin's side, and so they try to make the gulf between man and animals as wide and deep as possible Some would prefer to say that animals were senseless, automatic machines, without any rights or sense of feeling, rather than to admit that they have immortal souls. But no man should be so self-important as to dispute God's right to give to other animals physical and mental functions in any degree or kind that His omniscience may choose.

Rev. Dr. Fulton says on this subject, "I must now carry this thought very much further by laying down a large proposition. It is simply this, that a clear recognition of the near relation of man and beast in the Divine work and purpose of God belongs to the very foundations of the Christian religion, and is plainly asserted in Holy Scripture from the creation of the world until the proclamation of final redemption in Christ." So far as my feelings are concerned, I am proud to acknowledge that the Creator of animals is my Creator. Infinite wisdom forms no creature of any kind that is not fit to excite admiration for the Creator. This is true of any one of the least of the productions of divine wisdom and therefore must be so of all.

Man's elevation in the scale of perfection should not cause him to despise the inferior works of nature and look upon them as mean and insignificant. Neither should he take offense at the humane-doctrine which teaches a continuation of their existence, because they seem low and small in his estimation. He should blush to entertain such sentiments when he reflects that life, in all creatures, is a precious possession, and that He who made man made every other living being, and He cannot entertain a mean opinion of any creature without some reproach of the wisdom which conceived it. If it was not beneath the dignity of heaven to create the most diminutive animal it cannot be unbecoming in the same power to continue its existence.

If inferiority is a sufficient reason for excluding animals from an interest in futurity, it will prove as much with respect to man who is far inferior to the heavenly hierarchy.

Take the Fuegean and Hottentot who live in caves go naked, and eat lizards, and snakes, and what do they know or care about a New Jerusalem, a city of many mansions, with streets paved with gold? Now if God made a provision for animals when they were first created, and endowed them with happiness, and if He restores the lowest fallen man to mansions and gold-paved streets, why shall He not restore lower animals to green fields, running brooks and shady groves?

The teaching of religious philosophy has been hampered by creeds and dogmas and the fear of public criticism. We should not be jealous of science, but should exercise reason in determining philosophical truth. We should not close our eyes and turn away from scientific investigation because a few scientists are materialists.

According to Darwin's theory it required a miracle to create the four or five first beings, would it not have been just as consistent with the omniscient wisdom of God to have created all according to the narrative given in the Bible? The formation of some new species by the union of those standing in the nearest natural relation to each other is absolutely prohibited by the laws of nature which pass the sentence of sterility upon all hybrid offspring.

Neither can the theory of natural selection produce new forms, but can only select from the forms already in existence. If new species are created out of the union of old ones, we should expect to find creatures in every stage of progress; but instead we find an empty space between each of the several orders, and between man and the animal next to him, a distinction which was never changed since creation.

Forms may be modified by selection, but no well substantiated new forms have ever been produced.

The researches of scientists, during the history of man, for six thousand years, have failed to produce a single instance. It is true the gradations between the higher species is well established by the laws of nature, yet the difference is so well marked that no doubt is left as to which species each belongs. This beautiful gradation is well marked throughout all creation. The scientific world is indebted to Mr. Darwin for many suggestive thoughts on this subject, but near resemblance does not furnish substantial proof that man descended from lower forms of animals.

On the other hand, this uniformity of design does furnish proof that all animals were created by one and the same Creator, and that each is endowed with a physical formation and mental faculties peculiar to its own species. This unity of design is founded on the most solid argument which the light of reason supplies for the unity of God; but the knowledge of the general fact on which that argument proceeds is not confined to the student of theology. It forces itself irresistibly on the thoughts of all who are familiarly conversant with the phenomena, either of the material or of the moral world; and is recognized as a principle of reasoning, even by those who pay little attention to its most sublime and important application.

There is an effort by some materialists to find the supposed missing link between man and the ape, but there cannot be any scientific reason for expecting to find a missing link between any of the species. Any remains of extinct animals which prove to be a separate species, simply adds one more species to the animal kingdom, and that is all.

M. Cuvier, a short time before his death, had formed a classification of extinct animals, and his collection of the species that are now lost to the world, amounted to about seventy, which would indicate that the theory of a missing link is not scientific to say the least for it.

Mr Darwin admits himself, that "the great break in the organic chain between man and his nearest allies cannot be bridged over by any species."

Evolutionists fail to establish theories of a permanent and tangible nature. They go back to the origin of forms and attribute a starting-point to the laws of nature, ignoring the fact that there cannot be a law without a law-giver. There must be an intelligent First Cause to make such laws and keep them in force. Taking these indisputable facts into consideration, the revealed description of creation is most consistent with the divine nature of God, and the only system which has survived and will survive all the combined criticism of the scientific world.

CHAPTER XII

CHEMICAL COMPOSITION OF ANIMALS —CRUEL ANATOMISTS

All animals composed of like substances—Subject to same emotions and influenced by like causes—A better day coming for their sad condition—God will hear their cries.

PHYSIOLOGISTS have analyzed the brains of man and of the lower animals and have found that there is no distinction either on the surface or in the interior of the cerebrum, cerebellum, medulla oblongata or spinal cord, as there is a continuous tract of the gray and white matter which is made up of an assemblage of ganglia which has no external or internal distinction. In man as well as in the lower animals the brain is a prolongation of the spinal marrow and the skull is the prolongation of the vertebral column.

Brain matter, like gold, is the same, it matters not where you find it or in what proportions, whether in man or lower animals, whether in large or small quantities.

The mysterious pineal gland, a small heart-shaped pulpy substance found in the brain, was formerly considered the seat of the soul by Descartes and others, but as it is found in lower animals as well as man, the hypothesis has been rejected for that reason.

Chemists have analyzed the brains of men and lower animals and have found that they are composed of carbon, hydrogen, nitrogen, oxygen, etc.

Now can these chemical compounds compose the splendid dreams of Shakespeare or the epic poems of Milton or the Iliad of Homer? Can a number of carbon, hydrogen, nitrogen, and oxygen atoms produce the various intellectual acts of a horse, a monkey, or a dog? Can such a chemical compound associate articulate sounds so as to understand language, obey commands, move at will, act from an impulse of love or hate, and possess the sensitive faculties of touch, taste, smell, hearing and seeing?

It cannot be conceived that a combination of material atoms can produce immaterial actions and thoughts It is plain that there is some agent prior and extraneous to the brain, which acts upon the mind, or soul, and thereby tells upon the physical system of animals. While the brain may be considered the organ of the soul it does not follow that the soul is the product of the brain.

No system of theology would dare to admit such an hypothesis For instance, take the water-wheel of a mill The wheel sets the machinery in motion, but it is not the motive power, as the motive power is the water.

So the brain will move the different faculties of the body but the motive power is the soul. Take the faculty of thought, and we see that it is not the product of physical forces, and cannot be developed like the gradual growth of the body, but is a spontaneous action guided by a spiritual force

A letter is brought by the postman to an individual; he reads it and the contents have such a wonderful effect on his nervous system that he drops dead. It was purely a mental action, as the man received some fearful and distressing tidings.

One friend calls upon another and informs him that some great catastrophe has happened to one of his nearest and dearest relatives, and as a result his friend may lose his sight or hearing or become paralyzed. Here the thought struck the man with a physical effect. Thought acts upon the brain, which acts upon the nerves, and they act upon the senses. In this way animals are often frightened to death without physical violence. The sense of nausea may be excited through the sense of sight. And by strong mental emotion vomiting may sometimes be produced.

If there is a pain anywhere in the body it may be intensely increased by thinking about it or diminished by a diversion of the thoughts from it. The history of martyrdom supplies a multitude of instances which perfectly demonstrate the power of the soul over the body. A certain Christian martyr told his friends he would lift his hands over his head just before death as a token of the triumph of his soul over the body. In the midst of the flames, the power of speech gone, the flesh all crisp so that his friends thought him dead, he suddenly lifted up both hands and clasped them together three times.

We read of a cruel anatomist who opened the abdomen of a dog, and while she lay in the most pitiful tortures offered her one of her young puppies, which she immediately began to lick and to talk to in her own language, and for the time seemed insensible to her pain. On the puppy's being removed, she kept her eyes fixed on it, and commenced a wailing cry, which seemed rather to proceed from the loss of her young than a sense of her own torment. We may well blush to contrast the cruelty of the man with the loving devotion of the dog. The greatest agony which the body can endure is sustained for the sake of love, which is the strongest faculty of the soul.

That the mechanism of the nervous system is governed by an independent, immaterial power is well established in the phenomena of the allied spiritual forces known as hypnotism, animal magnetism, and mesmerism, which proves that there is a spiritual nature in all animal life independent of the physical. All these spiritual forces can be conveyed by and to lower animals as well as to man.

Dreaming, which is common to both man and lower animals, is another proof that all animals have souls. Sleep is not the extinction but a suspension of some of the faculties which extend to the body. The soul continues its activity, and when the body awakes the two continue as before to act together.

Death is called falling asleep, which is an appropriate illustration as, in either case, it is not the final end of life. During sleep all the faculties of the soul may be in exercise. The body can hear, see, walk, utter sounds, and perform the several offices of life. When dreaming, the voluntary muscles are sometimes thrown into action, and the dreamer moves, groans, or cries. We often witness this phenomena of dreaming in dogs, cats, and other animals.

The soul while destitute of the control of the body, is often overwhelmed with a chaos of ideas, rushing upon each other with such rapidity that the transactions of ages are crowded into moments, and all kinds of intellectual fancies both possible and impossible are united together.

Difficult mathematical problems have been solved by a dreamer which could not be done while awake. A dreamer may hold an extended controversy with some one and recognize the arguments used by his opponent.

I believe many an individual has been conscious in sleep of brilliant thoughts that would make his name as memorable as that of Homer or Milton, if he could only embody and give utterance to them in his waking hours.

An infant will laugh and coo while asleep, and

we are told it is being entertained by the angels, which is probably true But I have observed the same manifestations in the faces of kittens, puppies, and other animals, and I must attribute the same phenomena of soul in the one case as in the other, which affords a strong ground for the assertion that lower animals possess an inward sense analogous to the faculty of man.

It seems to be a well-established fact that the mind or soul never does and never can exist without thinking. Hence while asleep the mind has ideas of memory, ideas of consciousness, ideas of imagination, and ideas of reasoning, which are some of the most important faculties of the soul, and are manifested in dreaming with as much prominence in animals as man. In dreaming, the vital force is independent of matter, and consequently shows that it proceeds from the faculty of the soul.

There is another state of the body which bears a close resemblance to dreaming, which is called reverie, in which the mind is so engrossed upon some particular train of thought that the person is oblivious to everything else. The attention may be so completely fixed upon one object that there is an insensibility to all other impressions connected with it, although everything which bears upon it may be in full view.   In other words, your mind may be engaged in one thing and your body in another.   You may be so intently engaged in the music of one particular instrument, of an orchestra, that you may not recognize the sound of any other instrument.

It is a demonstrated fact that every part of the animal system may safely sleep or become torpid except the soul and vital organs.

Nature has established a law that as soon as the vital or involuntary functions are discontinued, life ceases; the soul deserts the body, the laws of chemistry, hitherto held in subjection by a superior control, assert their authority; and the whole visible system falls a prey to corruption and ruin.   But the soul does not suffer with the body, in the destruction to which it is turning, but finding the latter no longer a suitable residence for it and no longer able to accomplish its purpose, wings its flight to God who gave it.

Then again it is argued that the soul is immaterial, and is superior to the physical organism from the fact that a person dying of old age will retain the mental faculties until the very last breath. Often we see the most astonishing powers of mind, the clearest discernment and judgment inhabiting a wretched, weak, and decayed body. Now if this argument proves anything for man's immortality it proves as much for lower animals who retain their mental faculties to the last moment when dying from injury, disease, or old age.

It often happens on the approach of death, when the body has really commenced to decay, that the soul is perfect in all its conceptions and oftentimes surpasses its greatest powers when in health.

Physiologists have been making unnecessary and cruel experiments on man and animals for the last two or three centuries to satisfy their morbid curiosities. They have dissected every part of the body which can be dissected while living, and every part of the body after death which could not be done before. They have caused every conceivable manner of torment that the devilish nature of a man could invent They have traced every nerve, artery, muscle, fibre, and vessel. They have tortured to death by mutilating, cutting, burning, hanging, and drowning by a gradual process; they have roasted, frozen, boiled, and skinned the poor

animals while in the full possession of the faculties
of their souls.   They have laid bare the nerves and
then burned them with currents of electricity which
is the most agonizing torture that can be imagined
All this has been done to learn something of the
phenomena of life, and what has been the result?
They have become so accustomed to material anatomy that they imagine that a thing does not
exist unless they can show it on the point of their
lancet or scalpel   Now can a materialist show an
idea upon the point of his lancet?   Or can he show
a thought on the point of his scalpel?   In measur-
ing the various parts of the body can he measure
off an inch of love, a foot of anger, or a yard of
jealousy?   Can he locate, in that innocent, bloody
piece of flesh before him, in the form of a dog,
where that true and everlasting love it has for its
master is to be found?

We are glad to know however, that a large majority of our best physiologists are not vivisection-
ists nor materialists, but believe that there is a
controlling agency or vital principle distinct from
the organization of the body, and are not guilty of
experimenting with the suffering of any living being.

Dr. J. L. Brachet, a cruel physiologist of Paris,

relates with a degree of pride and pleasure, some of
his experiments on animals which he defines as
" demonstrations in physiological science." He
speaks of how he tormented a dog by sticking it
with needles placed in the end of a rod, and at the
same time scolding and shouting at it to arouse its
anger. He would retire for a short time and then
return and repeat the experiment until, as he says,
" The animal became furious whenever it saw me,
so I put out its eyes. I could then appear before it
without the manifestation of any aversion. I spoke
and immediately its anger was renewed. I then
disorganized the internal ear as much as I could,
and when intense inflammation made it deaf, then
I went to its side, spoke aloud and even caressed it
without its falling into a rage."

Now this " demonstration in physiological science " can be made to demonstrate several important facts not intended by Brachet. In the first
place, no doubt, the dog had been, up to this time,
as kind and affectionate as a child. It had been
the household pet of some kind family and the
loving and trustful companion of some devoted
child, but was caught away from home and unfortunately fell into the hands of an inhuman mon-

ster. As Brachet proceeded to torture the poor,
innocent animal, it stood it patiently as long as it
could, and then began to show its disapproval, as
best it could, by uttering objections in its own
language against such treatment. This was nothing more than would result in a human being
under like circumstances. " The animal became
furious when it saw me," says Brachet   And why
not ? A kind, affectionate, sensitive animal be-
trayed, scolded, and tortured without any reason or
excuse, why should it not recognize that hideous
face and hellish voice and " become furious " at his
approach ? Then says Brachet, " I put out its
eyes." He could then slip up close to it, but as
soon as the poor dog heard his voice " its anger
was aroused." It is plain to see the reason, all the
way through the experiment, why the dog was distressed and cried out with a protest at his presence.
It had been tortured from the beginning without
offering it any kindness. Brachet again seized and
bound the dog and thrust an iron instrument into
both ears and rendered it deaf. He then approached
its side and shouted but it made no demonstration.
What a wonderful " demonstration in physiological
science," that a man should shout to a poor blind

and deaf animal without attracting its attention.
But the saddest part of the experiment is yet to
come.   Up to the time he put out its eyes and destroyed its hearing he had never offered it any
kindness, but after this cruel work he says he
" caressed it without its falling into a rage."   Now
just think for a moment of the action of that dog
at the first offer of kindness through all that intense agony.   Here was an affectionate, forgiving
nature in that poor, bleeding, blind, and deaf dog
which seems more like the nature of Deity Himself
than an animal, as it exhibits a virtue far superior
to the nature of man.   After that incarnate fiend
had done all of his bloody and cruel work, the poor
dog was ready and willing to make friends and
kiss the murderous hands which had caused its slow
torture to death   But the dog and the man have
long since been dead, and now comes the question,
where are their souls ?

What kind of justice, love, and mercy would give
the soul of that man an eternal home in heaven
among the good, merciful, and pure, and doom the
soul of that loving and forgiving dog to an eternal
annihilation ?   All nature shrinks from such injustice.   There is something in the idea of annihilation

of a poor, helpless, innocent being so appalling to human nature that it withers up all that is generous, hopeful, and noble in man's nature. To think that when some poor animal has suffered all the abuse and torture its sensitive nerves can bear and then when the icy hand of death forces the struggling life away, it is lost in the dark and dismal tomb of annihilation, would freeze the very heart of a sensitive human being and spread over his nature the most sad and dismal gloom imaginable.

Every kind of being as well as man, was created for the glory of God. Alas, then, that there should be so many heartrending scenes spread out before us, scenes so terrible that the liveliest imagination cannot portray them nor the most gifted tongue describe them Everything in the great cosmos was created and designed for some special purpose or else we impeach God's omniscience and omnipotence. I wish to make plain the incontrovertible fact, by what we see and know of the phenomena of nature, that nothing is low, nothing little, nothing in itself unworthy, in the view of the great Creator and common Parent of the universe; that nothing is beyond the reach of His benevolence, or the shadow of His protection.

God alike supplies the wants and ministers to the enjoyment of every living creature; He alike finds them food in rocks and in wildernesses, in the bowels of the earth, and in the depths of the seas.

His is the wisdom that to different kinds and in different ways, has adapted different habits and modes of being, and has endowed each with an intelligence sufficient for existence. If the inanimate matter which forms the universe exhibits design and purpose it must follow that the animate or higher forms of creation have a higher and nobler purpose in creation. When we look up to the sky, as the orb of day is gilding the whole horizon, we at once discover that the Father of the universe designed it to diffuse light and heat; when we look at the hills and the mountains, we think that they were placed there to attract the humid clouds that float through the atmosphere so that the fertilizing streams might descend upon the earth; when we look at the great expanse of stars each of which is a sun surrounded by worlds, we think of the future provision the All-wise Creator has made for poor suffering animals. In short, when we turn our attention to the various parts of creation we must recognize that all are framed for a purpose by the Creator.

We cannot suppose that lower animals, the fairest and noblest of all God's creation, except man, with bodies and powers capable of development and possessed with affections and gratitude more durable and faithful than man, are soulless. In the mighty plan of the infinite mind a higher object than that assigned inanimate matter, has been assigned animals and we believe that God in His wisdom and justice has caused to dwell within every living creature a soul whose duration of existence no limit can be assigned. Everything I have learned of the Creator leads me to believe that there must have been some other object in view when He created animals. He did not intend them to pass through this world in sorrow and suffering with the end doom and annihilation. It would be to say that God created all things and then gave an eternity to the heavens, earth, and man, but left the lower animals alone of all His creation to be annihilated.

Look at the little bird, that shakes its beautiful plumage; spreads abroad its wings; soars joyously aloft, and there floats in the blue heavens above us, and sings its sweet song of praise to God who made it. There is exquisite grace in the form of that precious little body; there is supreme wisdom displayed in its structure and plumage; consummate benevolence manifested in its intelligence and happiness, and the melodious song it sings was taught it by the Great Teacher of all things. Yes, Nature tells us there is a Creator who will not annihilate His creatures. We see God in everything around us. In the moon we discover His purity; in the sun His glory; in the abundance of autumn His benevolence; in the lightning's flash His power; and in His long patient dealings with man His infinite love.

Must we think otherwise of His justice? For six thousand years the whole creation has been groaning and travailing together in pain and sorrow.

When shall we look for the day of deliverance for suffering animals which form the largest part of creation? We think the time is near "when the desert shall become a beautiful field, and the fruitful field be accounted for a forest and the spirit of the Lord shall be poured out upon them." For the animals which are in darkness and suffering a better day is dawning.

The morning is already beginning to break upon the mountains. The voice, not of one, but of thousands is heard in the wilderness saying " prepare ye the way." In the whole history of God's ways we cannot find a single instance of His failing to do justice—not from the hour of the transgression of Adam and Eve—not from the flood—not from the promulgation of the law from Mount Sinai, when the thunder and lightning gave awful demonstrations of His authority—not from the entrance of Israel into the promised land—not from the terrible period when the Jewish economy was swept away and the nation destroyed—and not from the agony on the cross when all creation was promised eternal life.

Justice to animals will come. God does not delight in the suffering of His creatures but His justice must be vindicated, and thus it is that the mercy of the gospel mixes with the letter of the law.

His delight is in the happiness of that eternal nature which He Himself has formed, and except it be to the injury of those high moral attributes, He ever rejoices in scattering the fruits of His benevolence over the grateful and rejoicing family of His creation.

CHAPTER XIII

INFELICITY OF ANIMALS —THEY POSSESS A MORAL SENSE

Some animals have been the companions of man from the beginning of creation and will follow him to his final destiny—Man and lower animals will be restored to a new Garden of Eden.

ANIMALS are liable to infelicity as well as man, and as it is one of the chief arguments in theology that there must be a future for man in order that he may be recompensed for the miseries of this life, so we would reason for animals.

Animals have their dark hours of distress and silently and patiently suffer many sorrows mentally as well as physically. They suffer from disease, injuries, abuses, various wants and all kinds of cruelties inflicted upon them by man. They finally languish and die in agony, like the beings that are above them.

And yet for all this we are told by some that they have no share in a future life. If such is the case then we must conclude that they were produced in an evil hour and a fatal moment; for it appears as if the principle of sensibility, in a world where evil predominates, is a huge misfortune, and an ungracious gift, provided the creatures endued with it have no interest in the benefits of a better life.

To bring a being into a state of unmixed happiness, in any degree, can be no injury to it; or into a state of unmixed happiness, provided the happiness certainly overbalances the contrary, and the unhappy or suffering part be not greater than the being would prefer in order to obtain the happiness rather than lose it.

Nor can any wrong be done by producing a being subject to more misery than happiness, if that being has it in its own power to avoid the misery, or so much of it as may leave the remainder of misery not greater than what it would rather sustain than miss the proportion of happiness. The only case then, by which wrong can be done in the production of any being, is where it is necessarily and unavoidably made miserable without any recompense or balance of that misery; and such a case is so grievous, so utterly inconceivable to all reason, that the heart of a reasoning and considering man can scarce bear the thought of it.

Now, we well know that there are millions of beings whose grief and suffering have far outweighed all their enjoyment, and who have not been able, either by their innocence, their appeals and cries, or any power in them to escape their sad fate.

Then how can we acquit the justice and reasonableness of a Creator upon whom these poor creatures depend, and who leaves them such great losers by their existence, if there be no future state where proper amends may be made?

Is it reasonable to suppose that the man whose hands are all stained with the blood and cruel tortures of some innocent, helpless creature and whose life has been full of plenty and grandeur, shall at death, be wafted to the skies and admitted to an eternal happiness while the poor victim of his torture shall be blotted out of existence?

To suppose such a case is to suppose such a constitution of nature, as can never flow from a principle of reason and justice.

That man and lower animals have a common destiny we believe is established by historical facts.

They are classed together throughout the Bible from Genesis to Revelation.

Lower animals suffered with man in the fall.
They have perished with him in deluges, in confla-
grations, in famines, in pestilence, in destruction of
wars and have been his constant companion from
the day of his and their creation   As they have
attended man through all his history they will also
attend him in his final deliverance and be restored
when he is restored, and have a place in those
happy regions, where nature shall reassume the
splendor and elegance of primeval beauty, in the new
world which God has prepared for all His creatures.

The attributes of God point out a continuation of
that mighty chain of living beings, which is the
astonishment of all contemplative minds.   And
must there not be a huge chasm, and a vast defect
in the great cosmos, if all nature is to be radically
destroyed below man?   Must there not be wanting, on this hypothesis, myriads of creatures to
testify the excellence of the Creator?   What can
exhibit the perfection of infinite life, but the communication of all possible degree of it; of infinite
goodness, but the gift of all possible degree of happiness; and of infinite power, but all possible
varieties of beings, which can be conceived or
imagined ?

We can look no way now without meeting the instances of the greatness of the Deity; and will there be fewer testimonies of His perfection in a better world? If anything is certain, it is that the perfection of God will never be less visible in His works in the future than they are at present. Though the ills of this world are very unequally divided, yet we have the consoling thought that amidst all the calamities and miseries with which we are surrounded there may be a bright hope of a better world where all pain is excluded and the souls of all God's innocent creatures are in a state of perpetual peace and happiness This undoubtedly is the most consistent view that any system of theology can offer for the sad cosmical derangement of creation, and the only system which can compensate for the suffering of the innocent and give to the Creator the attributes of justice and mercy.

I wish to plainly express my convictions on this subject. I believe, with the great teacher, St. Paul, that "salvation is made perfect through suffering." God's communicative goodness is always the same, and as His benevolence is eternal, He will continue to impart His blessings beyond the fleeting period of the present time, in after ages forever. The ways and works of Divine Providence are not all clearly revealed, and yet, a contemplation of them, though now they are wrapped in clouds and darkness, is the source of much pleasure and furnishes many noble arguments for praise and reverence.

If this is the case now in the contemplation of the works of creation, what will it be when all the secrets of nature are unfolded, when every creature which God has made becomes a recipient of blessings, as they did on the day of their creation in primeval innocence, when

> "Man, beasts, and bird, yea creatures all,
>   No longer curs'd for man's sad fall,
>   In chorus join'd shall voices raise,
>   To sing their lov'd Creator's praise "

That animals have a moral sense has been proven in so many different ways that it is no longer doubted. Some animals may not reach to the high point of the requirements of modern theology, but they do recognize a sense of right and wrong. When we compare that intense unselfish love and worship a dog will show for his master, and how trustfully he will look up to him as a superior being, to that of the worship of an idol by the Hottentot, we see a religion in the dog which approximates nearer the Christian religion than that of the savage. The dog worships a living, intelligent being, possessed of a soul, while the savage worships objects without life or sensation, such as wood or stone. Thus when we compare the moral sense of the most intelligent and kind animals, such as the horse, dog, elephant, and other of like good disposition, to the low and degraded types of man, there is no question that the lower animals practice a superior form of religion. We often see lower animals rising to a higher grandeur than man. "Love your enemies" was one of the most beautiful lessons taught by Christ, and yet we see it practiced in the lower animals to an extent never attempted by man.

The birds praise God as they "sing among the branches." And as St. Francis says: "There is no degradation in the dignity of human nature in claiming kinship with creatures so beautiful, so wonderful, who praise God in the forest even as the angels praise Him in heaven." There are animals which would sooner starve than pilfer or steal under the greatest temptations, there are some invariably true to their attachments, that show affection and profess friendship which nothing but death itself can dissolve.

Animals could not be domesticated without a conscience to direct them in matters of right and wrong. Without it a dog could not be true, faithful, and responsible for his acts.

A dog will often resist abuse from a grown person which he would allow in a child without any attempt to protect himself.

A horse will allow a child to crawl beneath him and cling to his legs without making an effort to dislodge or hurt the child.

The huge elephant by kind treatment becomes so gentle and true to man that he restrains his great strength and allows himself to be led by a child and will step aside to protect it.

Animals' sympathy and love for each other show a moral sense. They will defend each other against an enemy. Birds have been known to feed their blind, helpless, wounded, and orphaned. It is a pitiful sight to see a poor mother cat go hungry herself in order to feed her babies But even if animals have no knowledge of right or wrong, that does not change their chances of immortality any more than the case of an infant, idiot, or heathen.

Neither man nor lower animals are immortal by any choice or knowledge they may have on the subject. It is a direct gift from the Creator to His creatures, and He cannot give it to one without giving to all, unless He is partial in His beneficence. It is certain that the future life of animals cannot be absolutely denied without impeaching the attributes of God. It reflects upon His goodness to suppose that He gave to animals their sensitive nervous systems; intellectual capacities for love, devotion, and happiness and then subjected them to pain and sorrow without recompense. It reflects upon His wisdom that He should form them for the miserable duration of a moment, without leaving Himself the power to extend their existence, or to better their condition. It reflects upon His love, that He should expose them to the horrible evils of nature, and the cruel treatment of superior beings, which a tender disposition would be concerned to remedy or prevent. It reflects upon His justice, to suppose that He would destroy without a recompense, creatures that He had brought into a state of infelicity and capacitated for everlasting happiness. All of these conditions would reflect upon God's attributes did He not place all His creatures under the same immutable law of immortality.

But it is consistent to believe that God raised this mighty frame of things, in His great cosmos, in order to diffuse His goodness and display His glory. He conferred life and sensibility upon an infinite variety of creatures, with a view to their happiness, and gave existence to all the amazing diversity of forms in the universe, in order that His power and wisdom might be known, and made a provision for the restitution of all creatures to primeval peace and happiness in order that His love and justice might be manifested throughout all creation. Notwithstanding the diversity of creation among men and lower animals, all will have such places allotted them in the future world as are best suited to their respective natures and capacities. Their capacities will be extended and enlarged, in order to equalize the differences in this life. The weak and undeveloped will be made equal to the greatest and all will advance together in a uniform grade to a higher state of perfection.

In man there is an undeveloped nature, and it matters not how great his attainment, there are still capacities for greater attainment His full development is reserved for a future state. As about one-fourth of the human race die in infancy, their powers must be developed in the future state if they ever become rational beings. If the dormant mind of a savage or an idiot ever becomes sufficiently developed to enjoy a future existence, it must undergo a spiritual growth in the future life.

Therefore it is reasonable to conclude that all beings are in an embryotic condition, and require another life to complete their permanent existence. That lower animals have undeveloped and incomplete capacities requires no argument, and that their lives are merely embryotic and that this germinal beginning will be developed in a future state is as true as that the capacities of a child, an idiot, or a heathen will undergo a spiritual growth in the future state. As there is no waste in nature and all beings are endowed with certain abilities and capacities for life and happiness, if by any cause such endowment cannot be realized, then there must be a future state in order that they may be fully developed and enjoyed.

It is evident that God intended to confer upon

all His creatures a uniform degree of happiness when He gave them life and sensibility and pronounced them all " very good."

CHAPTER XIV

FUTURE ABODE OF ANIMALS — A PLURALITY OF WORLDS

A new heaven and a new earth—It is to be a place and a country—Many worlds awaiting to be inhabited by poor fallen animals—Room for all

TAKING it for granted that animals have immortal souls and share with man a future life, the question naturally arises, where is to be their eternal abode? There are some subjects on which we are obliged to exercise faith in connection with evidence. Such are the subjects of time, immensity, space, pure incorporeal intelligence, infinity, matter created out of nothing, innumerable systems of worlds, innumerable orders of beings, and a future life.

There may be primal causes as they appear to us which are the effects of other causes that are invisible. We sometimes know that such a thing will have such an effect, or that such an effect is produced by such a cause, but the manner we may not know.

The innumerable instances of things which seem

213

to be created with reference to certain ends, and
things which are propagated and repeated by the
same constant methods, are enough to convince us,
that there are ends proposed and rules observed,
which we do not see or understand.

The Bible plainly describes a real place for the
eternal home of all His creatures, and I often wonder why people try so hard to make heaven so
ethereal and mystic, when the inspired writers
made such an effort to make it plain that it is material in its nature. The Bible tells us that it is a
solid expanse, over which rests the throne of God
supported by the mountains as its pillars; which
makes it plain that there is a real place or world
beyond the starry firmament where all life is to be
continued.

The Bible teaches that there is to be a general
resurrection of all bodies and that the bodies and
souls shall again be united to dwell forever together
in eternity, and that could not be the case without
some natural and material paradise or original
Garden of Eden for their abode. We cannot conceive of bodies existing except within some definite
and circumscribed limits, as they must of necessity
occupy a definite and limited portion of space.

Enoch and Elijah entered the heavenly world both soul and body. Job says that after his body is destroyed, "in my flesh I shall see God."

The exterior nature of Christ's humanity must be located in some particular part of a visible and tangible world. How earnestly did St. Paul, during his suffering, long to "depart and to be with Christ, which is far better."

We know not in what part of the wide universe the throne of God is built and the eternal temple stands, but that it is a place and not a state the Scriptures lead us to believe. It is described as a "better country" free from all evil both of soul and body. Christ tells His followers, "in My Father's house are many mansions; if it were not so, I would have told you. I go to prepare a *place* for you" St. Paul says "Jerusalem which is above is free, which is the mother of us all."

It is represented as the "city of the living God, the heavenly Jerusalem," "Mount Sion," "the joy of the whole earth." St. Paul speaks of Abraham sojourning "in the land of promise, as in a strange country, dwelling in tabernacles with Isaac and Jacob, the heirs with him of the same promise, for he looked for a city which hath foundations, whose builder and maker is God," and further on he says, " here we have no continuing city, but we seek one to come."

In the book of Revelation, St. John gives a minute description of a material heaven, and says, "The foundations of the wall of the city were garnished with all manner of precious stones . . . And the twelve gates were of pearl; and the streets of the city were pure gold . . and it had a pure river of water of life, clear as crystal . . and on either side of the river were twelve kinds of fruits."

St Peter says, " We look for a new heaven and a new earth where dwelleth righteousness." St. Paul in speaking of the saved, says, " But now they desire a better country, that is, a heavenly : wherefore God is not ashamed to be called their God ; for He hath prepared for them a city." So it is reasonable to conclude that God has prepared a " place " and a " country " for the future abode of all His creatures.

Whether man and lower animals will occupy the same place does not enter into the question of the immortality of lower animals, as that matter rests with the Creator, and not with man. But the

Bible teaches us that animals were created long before man, and since man's creation they have been inseparably linked together from the first day of his creation to the mythical future spoken of by St. John, when he saw in heaven "round about the throne the beasts and the elders and the number of them was ten thousand times ten thousand, and thousands of thousands"

The word earth means our own world, the planet which we inhabit and the space around the heavens. The Bible tells us there are three heavens, the first, second, and third The first is the atmospheric heaven, or the expanse; the second is the astronomical heavens, comprising the stars and planets; and the third is the highest heaven, the throne of God and the home of the heavenly hierarchy and all spiritual life, for "the Lord hath prepared His throne in the heavens, and His kingdom ruleth over all."

It is evident the Creator has used a uniform gradation in all the things visible to us, and we must conclude that it is extended beyond our vision. The existence of an effect infers directly a cause. Every just consequence is founded on some known truth, by virtue of which one thing may follow from another.

It implies no contradiction or absurdity, from what we see and know, to say that there are probably many beings invisible and superior in nature to us. Since it has been proven by philosophers that all corporeal motions proceed originally from something incorporeal, it must be as certain that there are incorporeal substances, as that there is motion.

So there may be above us beings of greater power, and more perfect intellects, and capable of more wonderful things, who yet may have corporeal vehicles as we have, but finer and invisible.

The great complex system of our earthly planets, satellites, and comets, which revolve around the sun, is only an infinitesimal portion of the myriads of like systems which are composed of the same substance and regulated by the same laws which the All-wise Creator has made for some purpose. When looking up on a clear night and beholding the bright sky with such a glorious galaxy of stars, how few realize that those bright stars are suns which are the centers of solar systems of worlds; satellites and comets like our system, majestically sweeping around in space, all created and controlled by the omnipotent laws of God.

As we view this great expanse of the heavens and extend our view as far as we can with our natural eyes, we know that there are still worlds beyond, for we call in the most powerful telescope to our aid, and in proportion to its power we see myriads more, till at length, we resign ourselves to imagination and in the confusion of our thoughts and the weakness of our language, we speak of space as being filled, and of matter as being infinite.

Our conception of the number of stars is wonderfully increased by the consideration that each fixed star is a sun like our own glorious orb, and each the centre of a system around which other worlds revolve. Instead then of only one sun and one world in the universe, the science of astronomy has discovered to us suns upon suns, systems upon systems, and worlds upon worlds, dispersed through boundless space, and that our world would be no more missed from the countless millions rolling in ethereal space than a drop of water from the ocean.

Astronomers classify the stars by calling the most conspicuous "of the first magnitude." But few persons can see any smaller stars than the fifth magnitude. The ordinary telescope shows faint stars down to the tenth, while the most powerful instruments reveal those as low as the twentieth. The same process increased in power would demonstrate that still beyond the vision of man, and the most powerful telescope are myriads of stars filling the purpose for which God created them.

But let us notice our own solar system more minutely. We have seven large planets, or worlds, beside the earth, and about two hundred and thirty-five smaller ones, and twenty moons belonging to our system. Each planet is a world in common with ours and governed by the same laws.

They receive light and heat from the sun, and they have their satellites or moons which revolve around them. They revolve upon their axis and have their days and nights and seasons. They have their clouds and moisture, and consist of the proper chemical constituents to support vegetable and animal life. The surface of some of these has been sufficiently examined by astronomers to reveal hills, valleys, mountains, rivers, lakes and seas. God works by the same laws in all of His creation, and the conclusion is obvious that our globe is a specimen of all the similarly placed bodies of space as respects its constituent matter and the physical and chemical laws governing it. We are the more

entitled to draw such conclusions, because there is
nothing singular or special in the astronomical
situation of our earth different from many other
planets.

From this hypothesis we conclude that as other
planets are composed of the same elements and
governed by the same laws with similar environments, they are capable of supporting vegetable
and animal life. But it is not so much a question
as to whether they are inhabited as whether they
can be. To deny that they can, would be to deny
the omnipotence of God. When He who "hath
made the heavens, the heaven of heavens, with all
their host, the earth and all things therein" desires more inhabitable worlds, He will create them.
God has all eternity wherein to do His work and
takes His own time for each process. "One day is
with the Lord as a thousand years" We are here
taught that the space which has intervened between
the present time and the period when man and
the lower animals were first placed upon the globe, is
but one of the units of a vast series of chronological
periods which have gone before, and which stretch
backwards into the abyss of immeasurable duration.
The same law of force and matter has been in use

throughout all the past ages, working out the great plans of cosmical arrangements, yet the process has been progressive and advancing.

The discoveries of modern astronomy lead us to the conclusion that certain progressive operations are going forward, analogous to those which appear to have been carried forward in remote ages, and many planets appear to be in stages of progress for becoming habitable worlds The appearance of new stars, the disappearance of others which had long shone in the heavens, and the gradual diminution of the light of others and the change which appears to be occasionally taking place on the surface of the sun and the various planets, along with other celestial phenomena, are indications of the progress towards the preparation of a "new heaven and new earth." Is it reasonable to suppose that these worlds which are greater than ours have been swung into existence for no other purpose than to occupy a useless space ? That they are placed in the heavens only to adorn and bespangle a canopy over our heads for mere ornamental purposes ? Would this be a reasonable conclusion of the goodness of God, when our earth is full of His creatures groaning and travail-

ing under intense suffering waiting to be redeemed?

Rev. Dr. Chalmers says: "Why then suppose
that this little speck, called the earth, should be the
exclusive abode of life and intelligence? What
reason to think that those mightier globes which
roll in other parts of creation, and which we have
discovered to be mighty worlds, are not also worlds
in use and in dignity? Why should we think that
the great Architect of nature, supreme in wisdom
as He is in power, would call stately mansions into
existence and have them unoccupied?"

Certainly we have no moral right to lower the
dignity of the Creator by supposing He has not
made a wise provision for the care and future
happiness of all His creatures.

Christ says, "O ye of little faith. . .   Behold the fowls of the air: for they sow not, neither
do they reap, nor gather into barns: yet your
heavenly Father feedeth them" Nehemiah says,
the "Lord hath made heaven, the heaven of heavens, with all their host, the earth and all things
that are therein, the seas, and all that is therein,
and Thou preservest them all"; Ezekiel says,
"Saith the Lord God, behold all souls are Mine";

and Job says, " In the Lord's hands is the soul of every living thing " These passages, if words mean anything, are conclusive proof that God does care for His creatures.

The Author of the material elements is also the Author of the structure of man and lower animals upon one general idea and governed by the same general law So we reason by analogy of the entire cosmical arrangement of the universe

When we observe our own earth with its great variety of mountains, hills, valleys, plains, rivers, seas, trees, and plants, and the many races of men and species of animals, we must conclude that the millions of other worlds are not a barren waste swung into space without a purpose.

Our earth takes its place in the series of planets, which series is only one of the numberless other systems forming one group. Hence we cannot suppose that there is any peculiarity about it which does not belong to multitudes of other bodies, in fact, to all that are analogous to it.

The solids, liquids, and aeriform fluids of our globe are all reducible into about sixty substances known in chemistry as elements. Science has fully demonstrated the fact that Mercury, Venus, Mars,

Jupiter, Saturn, Uranus, and Neptune are composed of like substances as our earth which is one in common with the others.

They have a resemblance to our earth in various ways. We can know of one that its surface rises into inequalities, that it swells into mountains, and stretches into valleys. Of another that it is surrounded by an atmosphere which may support the respiration of animals. Of a third, that clouds are formed and suspended over it, which may minister to it all the bloom and luxuriance of vegetation. And of a fourth that a white color spreads over its northern regions, as its winter advances and that on the approach of summer their whiteness is dissipated, giving proof that there are rains, snow, heat, cold, and seasons suited for vegetable and animal life.

Herschel says, "When we contemplate the constituents of the planetary system, they are bound up in one chain, interwoven in one web of mutual relation and harmonious agreement, subjected to one pervading influence which extends from the centre of the farthest limits of that great system, of which all of them, the earth included, must henceforth be regarded as members."

Newton says, " All the planets are composed of the same matter with the earth, such as earth, water, stone, etc."

Rev. Dr. William Whewell, one of England's greatest philosophers, in his latest work, in speaking of the satellites, says, " We then find that the shining points which we see scattered on the face of the sky in such profusion, appear to be of the same nature as the earth, and may perhaps, as analogy would suggest, be like the earth, the habitations of organized beings ; that the rest of the heavenly host may, by a like analogy, be conjectured to be the centres of similar systems of revolving worlds ; that the vision of man has gone traveling onward to an extent never anticipated, through this multitude of systems, and that while myriads of new centres start up at every advance, there appears to be no limit."

Sir David Bremster says : " Analogy strongly countenances the idea of all the solar planets, if not all the worlds in the universe, being peopled with creatures not dissimilar in being and nature to the inhabitants of the earth."

T. C. Simon, in his work, " Scientific Certainties of Planetary Life," supports the idea " That mere distance of the planets from the central sun does not determine the condition as to light and heat, but that the density of the ethereal medium enters largely into the calculations. Neither on account of deficient or excessive heat, nor with regard to the density of the materials, nor with regard to the force of gravity on the surface is there the slightest pretext for supposing that all the planets of our system are not inhabited by living beings with animal bodies like our earth."

Richard A. Proctor, one of the most profound mathematicians and astronomers of this age, has written a book in which he gives reasons for his belief in a plurality of worlds with living beings. In speaking of some of the planets he says: "But shall we recognize in them all that which makes our own world so well fitted to our wants, such as land and water, mountains and valleys, cloud and sunshine, rain and snow, rivers and lakes, ocean currents and wind currents, without believing in the existence of forms of life?

"They exhibit in the clearest manner the traces of adaptation to the wants of living beings such as we are acquainted with. . . . Processes are at work out yonder in space which appear utterly useless, a real waste of nature's energies, unless, like their correlatives on earth, they subserve the wants of organized beings." Of the stars he says: "We see that the stars are suns, around which revolve myriads of worlds; and that the natural phenomena, such as we are familiar with as due to the solar heat, must be produced in these worlds by the heat of their central sun; and there must exist vegetable and animal life."

Robert Chambers, author of "Vestiges of Creation," in speaking of the satellites, says: "We have to suppose, that every one of these globes is either a theatre of organic beings, or in the way of becoming so. Such an idea is in accordance with our general conception of the dignity, not to speak of the power, of the Great Author"

We see matter as originally diffused throughout our own globe, consequently we presume matter to be everywhere the same in other globes. Light, heat and moisture are universal agents and bear marked relations to organic life and structure. Vapor or atmosphere, heat and light, pervade throughout, as do carbon, oxygen, hydrogen, and nitrogen, which are the elements in vegetable and animal life. Now if the other globes have the same constituent parts as our earth, namely, heat, light, and moisture, and have the same rough surface, is it not reasonable to suppose that they abound with hills and mountains, valleys and plains, lakes and rivers, plants and trees, and could be made the homes of animals?

Then again, if this is a correct hypothesis, and applies to more than one globe, it might well apply to all. If it does apply to all, then we have countless millions of worlds to be a "place" and a "country," beyond the computation of finite minds, for the future abode of all animals.

When we contemplate the magnitude of the heavens, our entire solar system with several planets larger than our earth, we readily observe that our globe is infinitely small compared to the immensity of the great expanse of "the heaven of heavens."

So the matter of room does not enter into the question of the immortality of animals. It is true when we stop to contemplate the mighty host who have gone before, we become amazed at the number. Of the two hundred and fifty-two billions of human beings supposed to have lived on the earth since Adam, not more than one billion ever heard

of Christ, which would leave two hundred and
fifty-one billion on the same equality with the
lower animals so far as the Christian religion is
concerned. But not without hope. They are in
the hands of God with the promise that "Christ
gave Himself a ransom for all, to be testified in due
time."

CHAPTER XV

MAN AS GUARDIAN OF THE LOWER ANIMALS — MORAL DUTY TO BE KIND

Bible enjoins kindness—Many instances of cruelty—The cries and moans of poor suffering animals plead for mercy—Man is responsible for their sad condition.

In view of the common destiny of man and lower animals, and their equal sensibility to pain, it becomes evident that man, as guardian, is under a moral obligation to be kind and merciful to lower animals as well as to his own species. When man avails himself of the service of lower animals he should use such methods in the management of them as is in accordance with their intelligence, sensibility, and nature; and not have recourse alone to force, compulsion, and violence. If they should, now and then, show restiveness and opposition, or refuse to do as they should do, men should learn to make proper allowance for such obstinacy of temper by reflecting upon themselves as beings with inclinations of their own, and conscious frequently that they are not willing to do at the bidding of others.

Man should regard lower animals as being in the same dependent condition as minors under his government, and not put into his hands to be wantonly tormented, beaten, cut, shot, stabbed, and mutilated. For a man to torture an animal whose life God has put into his hands, is a disgrace to his species. Such a man ought to be ostracized from decent society.

It is lamentable that at a time when the world is possessed of so many superior advantages, when the men of to-day so far exceed former generations in the attainments of science, and when heaven itself has interposed to teach so many tender lessons of pity and compassion, that we should be compelled to witness the wanton cruelty which is practiced and which we are powerless to prevent.

Animals are every day perishing under the hands of barbarity, without notice, without mercy, famished as if hunger was no evil, mauled as if they had no sense of pain, and hurried about incessantly from day to day, as if excessive toil was no plague, or extreme weariness was no degree of suffering.

While it is clear that the lower animals have

many claims to consideration in the great economy of Divine Providence, and the same assurance of immortality, yet as stated in the preface, I do not urge this as an incentive for man to be kind and merciful to animals, for the obligation remains the same whether they have souls or not.

Their status as respects a future life does not annihilate suffering and pain. Pain is pain; it makes no difference whether in an animal, a man, or as endured by the Son of God.

Moralists and materialists base their standard of ethics upon the light derived from nature and reason, and upon this same basis we urge the kind treatment of animals by reason of the universal moral law of justice and of mercy. In doing so we defend the cause of that class of beings to which Nature, though she gave capacity for pain, denied the power of remonstrating, after the manner of men, against suffering.

Kindness to animals is not confined alone to Christians nor to Christian nations. The code of moral ethics as first taught by Gautama Buddha was equal, and in some respects superior, to that of any other religion at that time. This great Oriental philosopher taught gentleness, kindness, peace, harmony, philanthropy, love, and virtue, and abhorrence of vice, long before the Christian era, and was the first to repudiate and prohibit the horrible and useless ceremony of animal sacrifices.

Later on his religion became blended with Brahmanism, and as a result the Brahmanic sacrifices were abolished. It is a sad fact that at the present time this religion has somewhat degenerated from its original standard. Nevertheless it is still true that religious teaching in the Oriental countries is replete with injunctions to tenderness and kind treatment of lower animals.

The Buddhist Scriptures teach that "The practice of religion involves, as a first principle, a loving, compassionate heart for all living creatures. Because he has pity upon every living creature, therefore is a man called holy. That the slightest act of charity, even in the lowest class of persons, such as saving the life of an insect out of pity, that this act shall bring to the doer of it, consequent benefit. . . . All living things of whatsoever sort call forth compassion and pity as they shall always exist in the spirit" Crude as the religion of the Hindus appears, yet they teach a moral code of ethics towards lower animals which would make a suitable chapter in the creeds of the Christian church. The following is a sample of Hindu theology: "He who injures animals that are not injurious, from a wish to give himself pleasure, adds nothing to his own happiness, living or dead; while he who gives no creature willingly the pain of confinement or death, but seeks the good of all sentient beings, enjoys bliss without end."

Man does not occupy the highest position in God's creation, and can claim only a share of His attention. The distance between man and lower animals is but a span, compared with the difference between man and the heavenly creation.

Man forms a part only of the animal kingdom, and the Saviour has enjoined upon him to be merciful to all creation even as his Father in heaven is merciful. The Bible plainly teaches that if we expect mercy we must be merciful, not only to our fellow-creatures, but to all inferior animals. Every act of cruelty to animals as well as from man to man, is certainly offensive to the Creator of all beings. The lower animals look up to man for happiness as man looks up to God. In advocating the cause, then, of these creatures by which we are everywhere surrounded, in lifting up our voices in behalf of these beings that cannot plead for themselves, we are surely not overstepping the requirement of God who has enjoined upon us the duty of opening our mouths for them. It is a plain moral duty, and as Rev. Dr. Norman McLeod says: "I would not give much for the religion of any man or woman whose cat and dog were not the better for it." Anna Sewell, in Black Beauty, teaches the beautiful lesson that, "There is no religion without love, and people may talk as much as they like about their religion, but if it does not teach them to be good and kind to beasts as well as man it is all a sham."

Before his fall, man was given dominion or guardianship over all living creatures, but just what effect the fall had upon his relation to animals cannot be ascertained   There is one thing very obvious, that the lower animals, as well as man, are not enjoying all the happiness now that they once possessed. They are involved in sufferings consequent upon the fall of man, being committed to the same fortunes with us, and partaking with us of the privations, sorrows, and dangers which we have brought upon ourselves by our guilt and disobedience. We ought to take

pity on them the more on this account, and instead
of aggravating, diminish as far as we can the necessary evils of their lot.

Our own sorrows should teach us to sympathize
with the distress of others. The kindness of God
to us in our low and lost estate should, in like manner, induce us to have mercy on the creatures which,
without any blame of their own, are involved in
the consequences of our transgression. Man by
his superior intellectual qualities has assumed the
position of "Lord of earth," but the right to rule
is not the right to tyrannize. The notion that animals were created only for the use of a man is a
weak and unwarrantable conceit. They were created long before man, and would have been better
off if mankind had never been made. They were
the objects of God's creative love, and were made
to glorify Him the same as man, and to say that
man was given dominion or guardianship over them
to oppress and abuse them would be to reflect upon
the goodness and wisdom of the Creator.

Power, like every other talent and blessing, was
given to man to be exercised in justice and mercy.
Though he claims the right to take the life of animals it does not follow that it is lawful to inflict

on them unnecessary pain. It is inhuman and barbarous to prolong their suffering by carelessness, or for selfish purposes, or for amusement. Though man claims the right to destroy certain noxious animals, yet pity is due them also. To torture is unmanly; to tyrannize where there can be no resistance, is the extreme of baseness.

There is no sin so heinous, or one that has been so little noticed and condemned by good people, as that of cruelty to animals. It is true that the legislatures of some States, and the corporations of some cities have taken the matter in hand, and have made laws to prohibit some of the most prominent exhibitions of wanton cruelty; and societies for the same purpose have been organized and supported by some of the greatest and best men of our nation; yet this great and much needed reform is only in its infancy. We could recall the names of many who have given the better part of their lives to mitigate the cruelties practiced on animals. Is it not a brave and noble thing upon their part to have stood so many years between the oppressors and their quivering victims and to have borne so long the contempt and ridicule of a great majority of people who claim to belong to a Christian country?

All honor to those great benefactors. While it is true that we as a nation have made slow progress in educating people to believe that cruelty to animals is a great sin, yet it is not so common now as it was thirty or forty years ago. I remember when quite young going into slaughter-houses, and witnessing cruelties which have left an impression upon my mind never to be forgotten.

I do not believe that any man or woman of noble sentiment and sympathetic nature, unless hardened by familiarity with such sights, can look into a slaughter-house and see the agonies, and hear the dying groans, and see the display of trunkless heads of calves, pigs, cattle, and sheep, and the bleeding and partly flayed carcasses, or look upon the blood-stained apron of the butcher in his shop, as he uses his monstrous knife, without a shudder, and a feeling of self-condemnation in being accessory to this wholesale slaughter by using meat. In one sense it seems vain to talk about this murderous work being done humanely, and such are its effects upon the sensibilities of people that in some States butchers are not allowed to sit upon a jury in cases involving the life of a criminal. Captain Bruce, the celebrated traveler, relates scenes of cruelty in

Abyssinia that have not often been referred to, so repugnant are they to humanity, and yet practices of equal barbarity have been found in our own country It would be a tedious work to particularize the numerous instances and kinds of cruelty that our religious country is guilty of.

How often are we called upon to witness the abuse of the horse, the most useful and willing animal in the world. How often, reduced to weakness by age and suffering, after years of faithfulness, he is made to drag out a miserable existence, or is subjected to cruel stripes by reason of his inability to accomplish labors which in his more vigorous days he would willingly have performed. How many do we see on our highways wounded and bleeding, pushed on to a speed for which they are disabled How often do we see them struggling in vain with burdens beyond their strength, the patient victim of the most brutal outrages, lacerated by the lashing of their cruel masters, and goaded on to renew the struggle, till they fall prostrate on the streets in hopeless agony. Many times we see the poor old faithful horse, after he becomes too feeble to do the work of his cruel master, turned out on the common to die from starvation.

Plutarch teaches the Christian world a beautiful lesson on this subject in the following words: "A good man will take care of his horses and dogs, not only while they are young, but when old and past service. We ought certainly not to treat living beings like shoes and household goods, which when worn out with use, we throw away."

Are not the innocent and helpless birds, which, in the beautiful language of Scripture, "sing among the branches," stoned, shot, wounded, and murdered, to exercise the ingenuity of the youth? In reading the life of Rev. Dr. Channing there is one incident recorded of his early youth that impressed itself more upon my mind than anything pertaining to his personal habits, and yet it may be regarded by some persons as being of too little consequence to be mentioned. When he was a little boy, one day on his way to school, he found in a bush a nest full of young birds. As they opened their mouths and begged for something to eat, he gave them a part of his dinner. So every day he prepared some food for his birds. The old birds seemed to understand it and were delighted at his kindness. But alas, the evil hour came. One day he went to the nest; there it lay on the ground, torn and bloody,

and the little birds all dead; and the father bird
was crying on a bush, and the mother bird was crying on a tree, as if their little hearts would break.
Then little Channing tried to tell them that he did
not kill their poor little children, that he never could
do such a mean, cruel thing as that, but that it was
some wicked boy that did it. He said he tried to
feed them and help them along, so they might fly.
But it was of no use; he could not console them.
They kept on crying until this kind-hearted little
boy could not contain his feelings any longer, but
sat down and wept with such agony that he was
found and taken home in an unconscious stupor.
No wonder, that with such an early impulse
of kindness he grew up to be a man noted
for kindness of heart and a great religious
teacher.

While Abraham Lincoln was President, and during the darkest hours of the war, he was walking
in company with others near a hedge, and saw a
young bird fluttering in the grass near by. He
stopped, picked it up, and while he was walking up
and down the grove to find its nest, his companions
walked on, but the great and kind-hearted man continued his search until he found the place from

which the bird had fallen, and then gently placed the tiny creature in its nest.

How important that good people, who are anxious that the world should grow better, should honor and extol such noble traits in human nature

"Among the noblest in the land,
Though he may count himself the least,
That man I honor and revere
Who, without favor, without fear
In the great city dares to stand
The friend of every friendless beast."

Notwithstanding the rough and hard struggles in Martin Luther's life, he had a tender and loving heart above the average of most men. On observing a bird go to roost he made the following beautiful and tender remark: "That little fellow has had his supper, and is now going to sleep quite secure and content. Like David, he abides under the shadow of the Almighty, and lets God take care. How happy are the little creatures singing so sweetly, and hopping from branch to branch. We might well take off our hats to them and say, my dear Herr Doctor, we could not have learned thy art of trustfulness. Thou sleepest all night, without care, in thy little nest; thou risest joyful in the morning, and praisest God, and then seekest thy daily food.   Why cannot I, poor fool that I am, live like these little saints in the fulness of content and trust "

Almost every one seems to enjoy, to some extent, the destruction of life.   Some children at a very early age delight in such amusement.   They will catch flies and other insects and pin them to boards, pull off their legs and wings, and seem to enjoy their painful writhings and flutterings.   They are often taught by thoughtless parents the early use of whips, sling-shots and air-guns, and soon delight to torment and maim every creature they come in contact with.

While in college I was frequently called upon to witness the experiments made on animals by the hypodermic syringe, air-pump, electricity, and some of the most horrible and useless forms of vivisection.   Such cruelty ought to be prohibited by law. Men who claim to be teachers are lost to all sense of humanity when they practice such useless and barbarous experiments.   It is a miserable education for the young to behold poor creatures suffering with agony of the most horrible kind, for the purpose of making physiological demonstrations, which may be just as accurately made without the ex-

pense of suffering. The power which was given by
the Almighty to man for the protection of His creatures is frequently and wantonly used in torturing, where pity should prompt to an opposite
course.

The cries and moans of the poor oppressed creatures plead in a language too pathetic to be disregarded except by those who disgrace the name they
bear. "The beasts of the field," says the pathetic
voice of inspiration, " cry to Thee, and Thou hear-
est them," and surely those sufferings, unjustly inflicted, must ultimately call down the vengeance of
that Being whose ear is ever open to the cry of distress The voice of nature cries aloud against such
conduct. From the winged birds and insects of the
air, from the beasts and living things upon the
earth, from the harmless inhabitants of the waters,
there is a continued cry to God against the wrongs
they are made to endure. The man who unmerci-
fully abuses one of God's creatures without a
cause, is a disgrace to his species, a tyrant of a more
ignoble, but not less hateful kind, than he who
makes use of the privileges of a throne to molest
and injure his fellowmen. He sports with suffering
which is always sacred to the good; he oppresses

the defenseless, a cowardly action, and he gratifies his malignity, a fiendish principle of joy.

It is impossible for any one unless he is insensible as a stone to the sight of suffering, or wilfully shuts his eyes to the truth, to doubt for one moment the appalling statement, that man by his cruelty, and oppression, and injustice, has made himself the enemy of the whole animal creation. Why is it that almost every creature, with instinctive horror, shuns the approach of man? Is it not because the creature has been made to feel that man is his enemy, and that he is cruelly dealt with when he falls into man's hands?

It is related that when Prof J D Dana, the great naturalist, was on his voyage in the South Pacific seas, he landed on one of the coral islands which had never before been visited by man.

" He went ashore in the early morning, and beheld a scene of tropic loveliness, brilliant with beauty and abounding in life. A great flock of tall, white birds was on the beach, and as he walked towards them they looked at him with no fear and with nothing but a gentle curiosity.

" They never had been frightened by powder and the deadly sting of the bullet. They knew nothing

of the cruelty of man. He walked among them
and placed his hands upon their tall, downy heads
and necks, and stroked them as if they were pets
in his own family. Then he planned to kill one
and take it home for his museum; and selecting his
victim, he took out his pen-knife, and stroking the
head of the beautiful bird, pressed the keen point
through the white plumage into the neck until the
feathers were spotted with a single drop of blood.
The bird turned his head and looked into the great
naturalist's eyes with an almost human gaze of
wonder and appeal. The knife was withdrawn.
A deep fountain of pity and love opened in the
good man's soul, and he turned away and left
these innocent unfrightened creatures of God un-
harmed "

We call lower animals *wild* because they are intelligent enough to keep out of the reach of man
who is their worst enemy If they have never
been mistreated and are assured of man that he
will treat them kindly they will soon learn not to
fear him.

Deer, antelope, buffalo, swan, squirrels, and many
other animals that are wild in their native state, if
placed in a park and treated kindly will soon be-

come tame and gentle, and seem to really enjoy man's society.

Fish will flee from the approach, or even the shadow of man, but can be tamed and become so confiding that they will approach to the edge of the water and take food out of a man's hand

We read in the life of Robinson Crusoe that when he was shipwrecked and drifted ashore on an island where no human being had lived, he soon tamed all the animals so that they were his friendly companions. Whether this be true or not, yet the principle is true. The golden rule will work with animals, in most cases, as well as with mankind. All successful tamers of ferocious as well as domestic animals, are men who treat them with perfect kindness.

Almost any sin can say more for itself than the sin of cruelty to animals, as there is no temptation nor good reason why such a sin should be committed. As the lower animals have not the power of expression, and of complaining of their wrongs, we should not take advantage of their condition. The more helpless the object of oppression be, the greater the demand on our sympathies. We feel more deeply when injuries are done to the poor than when done to the rich. We feel more deeply when injury is inflicted upon the widow and the orphan, than upon those who are surrounded with friends, and in the midst of prosperity We feel more when injury is done to a helpless infant, than to a man in strength and vigor, and able to defend himself. Now, were mankind guided by this principle in regard to the lower animals, how careful they would be not to inflict cruelty, and how tender would be their treatment. When man is oppressed or injured, however so helpless, he can tell his wrongs, and point out the person who inflicted them. The poorest of the earth can publish the shame of those who grind their faces with oppression; they who receive unjust punishment can raise their voices against the guilty tyrants.

But the poor and often unpitied animals have not this power and this privilege. Though the barbarity with which they are treated be ever so cruel, they cannot complain of their merciless usage. With a sensibility to suffering as strong as that of a human being, they are doomed to submit to whatever man may inflict without the possibility of making it known, and without the aid

which sympathy and hope are fitted to inspire.

When men are called to endure agonizing torture it is seldom that they have not some one to
sympathize with their sorrows, and to do all that
tenderness and pity can do to alleviate their distress.

But the animals unsupported, unsoothed, solitary
and silent must bear their heaviest burdens and endure their greatest agony   There is no one to be-
stow upon them a word or look of pity.

It is impossible to estimate the obligations under
which we are laid to the animals, for the numerous
ways in which they minister to our happiness ; and
what I contend for is that these ministrations
should be secured with the least possible expense of
suffering. Animals doomed to slaughter should
be slain by the least painful and the least pro-
tracted process of dying; those subject to us
for labor should be treated with gentleness and
nourished with care ; noxious animals and those
that men have found it necessary to destroy, should
be destroyed without any uncalled for suffering ;
while the insects which flutter in the air should be
exempt from cruelty, and treated with mercy.   All
living things are objects of God's peculiar care.   If

the lower animals had not received an equal share
of God's kindness and compassion we might view
the subject in a different light   But instead of
there being condescension on the part of man
in showing mercy, it is seen to be only his Christian
duty.   On one occasion God spared a guilty city
from destruction, because it contained much cattle.
The innocence of the cattle was not only the cause
of the city being saved, but it helped to prevent
Nineveh from being destroyed with six score
thousand persons   This is one among many striking instances of God's care alike for man and
beast.   God said, "Every beast of the forest is
Mine, and the cattle upon a thousand hills.   I
know all the fowls of the mountains, and the wild
beasts of the field are Mine."

Man in his folly and in his pride, may imagine
that animals are beneath his regard, and that he, a
rational and immortal creature, may treat them
with contempt and with carelessness.   But such is
not the mind of Him who is good unto all, and
whose tender mercies are over all His works, and
who, though He listens to the praise of angels,
is not inattentive to the falling of a sparrow or the
cry of a raven.

God makes a plain statement in His word as to man's moral obligation to animals in the following passage, " A righteous man regardeth the life of his beast." This single passage most decidedly proves that it is a part of a Christian's duty to attend to the happiness of his own animals.

We have as much right to take this statement as a test of Christian character as any other statement in the Bible. It certainly cannot afford pleasure to a good man to see animals sacrificed as victims to cruelty for any purpose whatever, and the nature of man is nowhere seen in a more degrading light than when employed in exciting and superintending the brute combatants in the arena of animal warfare. I wish that it could be said that such scenes were known only in the dark ages and in barbarous countries. We despise the ambition of the conqueror who rides at the head of a triumphant army, when he aims at renown, by spreading around him misery and death, but how infinitely more contemptible are those laurels which are gathered in the contested fields of animal warfare, when the fierce antagonists grapple with each other, and one or both sink in the agonies of death. Most mean and cowardly employment! most un-

worthy of man, who has been provided with capacities for so much higher enjoyment in the fields
of mental and moral improvement. Besides this,
see the effect it has on the character of those who
are cruel to animals. If we look into the annals of
crime, we find that some of the worst forms of
guilt have had their origin amid such scenes. If a
man is cruel to animals it hardens his heart and
paves the way to cruelty to his fellow-men. He
who can unfeelingly look on any instance of suffering which his own hand or counsel may have
caused, has surely the capacity of looking with a
corresponding degree of insensibility, on the deepest agonies that can writhe the frame or the heart
of his fellow-creatures.

A man who unscrupulously vents his ill-nature
against animals will become severe, harsh, and even
savage in his dealings with his fellow-creatures. A
man who is cruel in his treatment of animals cannot be considered a safe and good husband, a kind
parent, a humane neighbor, or a gentle and tender
friend. Cruel and tyrannical to the poor defenseless animals, he will, of necessity, carry the same
temper into the relations and transactions of human
life, and be an offensive, a violent, and even a

dangerous member of society. Men cannot change
their dispositions like their dress, but whatever disposition they encourage will become habitual and
natural.

The wrath vented upon animals by beating is
a passionate and senseless wrath, like that which a
fretful, impatient man would show to inanimate
things. The inferior creatures often, have not
only to do the work of man, but to bear his spleen,
and endure his senseless anger. Men think there is
no evil in such actions because they can strike or maltreat an animal without its being able to make the
cruelty known, or without themselves being answer-
able to the laws of the country. But if the cruel
man appears so repugnant to all good people, how
does he appear in the estimation of that God whose
tender mercies are over all His works, and who has
given us a positive command that we must be merciful even as He is merciful? Is a man fit for heaven,
that holy, happy place, where there is nothing to
hurt or destroy, but where love rules in every
bosom and binds all the inhabitants into one band
of the most endearing and holy intercourse? Or
shall he not rather have his place assigned to him
with those dark and malignant spirits who delight

in misery as their proper work, and who are consigned to a state of congenial wrath, and enmity and despair ?

CHAPTER XVI

MEANS OF PREVENTING CRUELTY —AN EARLY HUMANE EDUCATION NECESSARY

Some of the forms of cruelty—Man should seek a better pastime than sporting at the sacrifice of suffering—Kindness is an indication of greatness.

LET us next consider some of the means by which the sin of cruelty to animals may be corrected.

As the propensity to cruelty often makes itself apparent in very early life, all who have the early training of the youthful mind ought to make it a distinct object of their care to check such tendencies. No parent or teacher can be considered as doing his or her duty who does not repress such tendencies by instilling better and wiser views of humanity Mark with displeasure every act of neglect and cruelty ; teach the children to view all living things as objects of God's care, and that He is interested in their happiness and displeased with any evil that is done to them Some leading views and predominant inclinations never fail to take

possession of the young while the mind is pliant
and flexible and these become habits and are
moulded into character, either virtuous or vicious.
It is the natural tendency of many children to be
cruel and to do all sorts of mischief; consequently if
the business of an early education was more thoroughly understood and proper restraints used to
prevent cruelty, there would be fewer criminals to
contend with

J. W. Cottrell, general superintendent of the
Detective Association of America, made the following statement: "With twenty-five years' experience as an officer, I know of but few criminals
who were taught to love animals, and searching
for the cause of crime, I find that the lack of humane education is the principal one."

George T Angell, President of the American
Humane Education Society, says: "Standing before you as the advocate of the lower races, I declare what I believe cannot be gainsaid,—that just
so soon and so far as we pour into all our schools
the songs, the poems and literature of mercy towards these lower creatures, just so soon and so
far shall we reach the roots, not only of cruelty
but of crime. A thousand cases of cruelty can be

prevented by kind words and humane education for every one that can be prevented by prosecution."

King Edward VII, in an address before the Royal Society to prevent cruelty to animals, made the following remarks: "The conductors of our educational establishments will more and more recognize that it is one of their great duties to imbue the mind of the young with the consciousness that, besides showing kindness and gentleness to their fellow-creatures, they ought also to show kindness and gentleness to the brute creation, to which we owe so much. The more this is taught, the more this feeling is inculcated, the more rapidly will the objects of this excellent society be accomplished, and the more certainly will the time arrive, as we hope it may, when the range of its duties and action will be greatly diminished."

Hence it is the business of a proper education to direct the young mind to a proper regard for the rights and happiness of all living things.

To instruct the youth in the languages and in the sciences, is comparatively of little benefit to the world, if they are not taught to be kind and law-abiding citizens. How often we see parents thoughtlessly place a whip, air-gun, sling-shot and

other destructive missiles in the hands of their
children and then encourage them to torment and
punish the innocent, confiding cat, dog, or other
domestic animals.

How little do they realize that they are paving
the way for a future criminal of some sort. A
want of thought on the subject is a far more common cause of cruelty than a positive depravity.
But a poison is no less deadly because it is taken
thoughtlessly than if taken designedly. A cruel
wrong committed whether by ignorance, delusion,
or thoughtlessness makes no difference to the injured as the suffering is the same.

The way then to make the world better, and to
abolish cruelty, crime, war and poverty, is by insti-
tuting a more humane and better system of education.

The various humane organizations mentioned in
the dedication of this book are doing a grand and
noble work by publishing and sending out millions
of leaflets, tracts, pamphlets, books and periodicals,
the object of which is to promote kindness and
prevent cruelty. Such humane literature should
be disseminated throughout the world, and all good
people should give the work their hearty support.

If we would save the structure of society from utter dissolution, maintain inviolate our civil and religious liberties, and preserve ourselves as a nation, we must teach and enforce humanity. This moral restraint should be taught from our pulpits, in our schools, and at our homes   And, especially should parents set the example, if they expect their children to aspire to kind and gentle disposition.

> " Ye, therefore, who love mercy, teach your sons
> To love it too   The springtime of our years
> Is soon dishonored and defiled in most
> By budding ills that ask a prudent hand
> To check them.   But, alas ' none sooner shoots
> If unrestrained, into luxuriant growth
> Than cruelty, most devilish of them all."

And above all things, do not crush out humanity by trying to ridicule a tender heart. I have seen men become angry, and have heard them abuse their wives and daughters because they were too kind-hearted to behead a chicken   How inhuman to abuse a person for possessing the noblest trait of character that God has given mankind.   Men may frown and ridicule, but angels will smile and Heaven will bless such sweet dispositions.

I was once sitting in a friend's house when a sweet, bright little girl came tripping into the room and said, "Papa, the cook wants you to please kill the chicken that is in the coop, as she hasn't the time to kill it." The gentleman told the little girl that he was busy also, and that she must go and kill it herself. She begged her papa not to compel her to it, for, said she, "I haven't the heart to kill the poor thing." Her father paid no attention to her reasons but compelled her to go out to commit the bloody work. She was gone but a few moments when she returned, weeping as if her little heart would break, and said, "O, papa, I can't kill the poor thing." The color came to his face, he arose in anger and dragged the little girl after him. I heard him give her several hard blows. Oh! how my heart ached. I would not have that single sin of trying to crush humanity out of that dear little girl's heart rest upon me, unforgiven, for the wealth of the universe. The enjoyment of my visit was destroyed, and after lingering long enough to kiss the merciful, precious little hand that would not take life, I left with a sad heart.

When we come in contact with a family that will pet and caress the animals about them, we feel we are in the society of good and kind people We like to hear a mother and father speak gently to their children, as considerate and loving parents will do On this same principle, to hear a person call a bird a "sweet little darling," a cat, a "dear little pet," a horse or dog a "nice, dear good fellow," etc., portrays a tender, loving disposition which goes to make a peaceful, happy home.

The peculiar lessons taught by Christ may in all cases be applied with the greatest power to accomplish the reformation desired. That great law of the Divine administration so distinctly pointed out in the words "blessed are the merciful; for they shall obtain mercy," ought never, for one moment, to be forgotten by any class of men.

Throughout the whole moral dominion, the rule may be considered as holding good, that the qualities which men display in their conduct, draw down on them a corresponding manifestation of blessings in the righteous dispensation of heaven. Those who, throughout all their conduct, show mercy to the whole family of the Creator, have a distinct assurance that they too, in their time of need, shall obtain mercy.

As in the societies of man, just and benevolent rulers, who maintain the rights and secure the happiness of their subjects, render their power more permanent and extensive; so every man who exercises his power over inferior animals with equity and kindness, best secures the benefit of their services. Subdued and attached, and rendered happy by kindness, they submit easily to his direction, and render, with ease and comfort, the services which are required of them. By not being irritated by abuses or injuries they are not tempted to inflict those severe retaliations which God, for their protection, has given them the means.

As the Creator gave to man, before the fall, a moral as well as an intellectual guardianship over lower animals, He gave also to animals a corresponding kind disposition in order that they might acknowledge man's superiority, and in this wise adaptation is found the source of various mutual blessings. Notwithstanding the sad derangement of peace and happiness which was the result of the fall, we yet see many animals clinging to man with a stronger attachment than they have for their own species. They seek his society and are delighted to be noticed, they rejoice in every mark of his approbation, and delight to be employed by him in services suited to their capacities.

Thus the comfort of man is evidently promoted when this dominion is wisely and justly exercised, according to the original design of the Creator A right to rule is not a right to tyrannize; and a right to service extends only to such duties as are consistent with the powers and capacities of the servant to perform.

All power is of God, and can only be lawfully exercised when exercised according to His design Power, like every other talent and blessing, was given to be exercised in wisdom and goodness, and according to the principles and rules appointed by Him who conferred it. The Creator has given to all His creatures the power of life, activity, and enjoyment.

He has provided for their wants, and afforded to them the means of happiness. He has, therefore, adapted external nature for their good as well as for man's; and has given to them their share of its blessings.

As their happiness depends so much on their environment, when under the control of man, how important that they should be treated with justice, goodness, and mercy. Is it not the very essence of benevolence to desire and to promote the happiness

of every being within the sphere of our influence?

Do not justice and rectitude require that we regard the rights of every living creature, and furnish
them a competence of sustenance and comforts
when we have deprived them of the means of pro-
curing it for themselves? Every place in the
Bible where God has revealed His will on this subject is distinguished for its tender care of the destitute, the afflicted, and the helpless.

The Bible enjoins kindness and compassion to all
the creatures placed under our power, in such instances as the laboring ox, harmless birds, rest on
the Sabbath, and relief of the distressed.

" Thou shalt not muzzle the ox that treadeth out
the corn," is a striking instance of minute attention
to the feelings and comforts of those humble ministers of good. We are thus taught the general
spirit we should cherish, we are specially taught
that every creature which toils for our benefit,
should receive a liberal participation in those blessings which we enjoy through their labors.

In the same spirit of compassion it is commanded,
" If a bird's nest chance to be before thee in the
way, in any tree, or on the ground, thou shalt not

take the mother with the young;" thou shalt not add to her wretchedness, that of losing her own liberty and witnessing the destruction or imprisonment of her offspring.

It was forbidden to yoke the donkey and the ox together, as they never associated together, and their tread was so unequal that it was considered a sin to compel them to be placed in the same yoke —a practical lesson which is ignored by many cruel masters at the present time.

The precept in the observance of the rest for animals on the Sabbath is a beautiful and impressive lesson which teaches man his moral duty to animals. The observance of this blessed day of rest belongs to the lower animals as well as man. "Six days shalt thou labor, and do all thy work: but the seventh day is the Sabbath of the Lord thy God: in it thou shalt not do any work, thou, nor thy son, nor thy daughter, thy man-servant, nor thy maid-servant, nor thy cattle (animals), nor thy stranger that is within thy gates" This blessed institution, appointed for man from the beginning of his existence; universal in the object which it celebrates, and the good which it is destined to advance; being suited to all beings of every country and every age, is justly denominated the universal holiday for man and lower animals.

It will suffice in this connection to notice one more important humane lesson taught in the Bible. " If thou seest the ass of him that hateth thee lying under his burden; thou shall surely help him." The natural principle of sympathy confirms the authority of this command, and shows its equity to every feeling mind. It requires us to relieve an oppressed or endangered animal and for fear the fact of its belonging to an enemy might be a less inducement, the command was made plain so as to remove that objection.

Every animal that may be in a situation of oppression or suffering is to be relieved, and that without regard to whom it may belong, though it be to our worst enemy. These precepts were given to teach humanity towards the inferior creatures; and if this spirit was recognized under the letter of the law in those early days, it must surely be made more in accordance with the gospel, which is so particularly a system of love and mercy under the Christian dispensation. The present time is proverbial for the advancement made towards a higher standard of be-

nevolence and charity so far as mankind is concerned.

Asylums have been established for the reception of
the wretched ; homes and hospitals for the children,
the aged, the friendless, and the afflicted , and the
streams of bounty have flowed copiously for their
support.

Individuals have called down blessings upon their
memory by the endowment of some charitable institution. Let any apparent want or distress of
mankind be presented to a community, and relief is
readily obtained But the uncomplaining, suffering
animal creation is often deemed an object neither
fit for compassion nor susceptible of feeling.

Many men in the name of charity have given
great fortunes to assist public institutions, some of
which practice vivisection in its most horrible
forms , and for every dollar thus spent, there is one
more groan, one more cry, one more quiver of the
nerves, and one more struggle in death's agony.
How often the means and power which a man possesses is given for purposes which cause untold suffering and agony when he might use such means to
make the world better and happier. How obvious
and important are these principles, yet how little

are they regarded and how slightly felt by multitudes professing to be Christians.

Like other important truths and duties, men acknowledge them, but they make little impression
on their hearts. Such a demoralizing effect of cus-
tom and familiarity with evil, and the frequent
abuse of power, and practices of the most odious
nature, which, if witnessed for the first time would
excite our terror, are daily beheld and committed
with the most heartless insensibility.

There is nothing more demoralizing to any people or country than the inhuman and barbarous
practice of sporting at the expense of animal life.
Man is the only animal on earth which kills for
fun, and in this respect is the meanest creature God
ever made. What are such amusements as cock-
fighting, dog-fighting, bull-fighting and pigeon-shoot-
ing but sports which are disgraceful to a civilized
people, fitted to foster the most baleful passions,
and to harden the heart against the calls of humanity?

What a peculiar sport it is to see animals harassed
with perpetual terror, brought together and compelled to fight a foe made so by man, and to witness
the struggle of death, and man shouting the louder

at the sight of the greatest suffering inflicted.
What kind of sport to a sensitive nature is it to turn
loose one bird after another, and then wound, maim,
and kill them in their attempt to seek their liberty
as they spread their beautiful soft wings and soar
towards heaven ?   When one is badly wounded and
makes a great effort to get beyond the reach of the
murderous gun, its writhing and struggles are
mocked by shouts and yells from the crowd present,
while bets are made as to the final results.

It does not seem possible that any kind-hearted,
benevolent man could derive any pleasure from beholding such scenes as these, if he would stop long
enough to reflect on the enormous evils of which
they are productive, and which have now become
so obvious and palpable as to draw forth the strong
and indignant protest of all kind and good men and
women.

The New York *Tribune*, speaking on this subject,
says : "The business is a detestable one, and should
be discountenanced by humane people and forbidden by law as absolutely as are any of the cruel and
degrading 'sports' of olden times.   The conflicts
of the Roman arena were less cowardly, for in them
the victims had at least a chance to fight for life.

Wanton, cowardly, and cruel in an inexcusable degree is the judgment to be passed upon this relic of
barbarism."

It must be far from giving any pleasure to a good
man, to see poor animals sacrificed as victims to a
love of amusement, or to gratify the idle curiosity
of unfeeling spectators. I wonder when men are
cruelly torturing harmless doves, if they ever think
that it was a dove that went forth from the ark,
at the bidding of Noah, and brought in an olive
branch as a token of the deliverance of man from
the flood, and that it was the form of a dove,
or an angel dove, which descended from heaven
as a means of ushering in the Christian dispensation.

David makes a pathetic plea against such sports
in the following words: "Remember this, that the
enemy hath reproached, O Lord, and that the fool-
ish people have blasphemed Thy name. O deliver
not the *soul* of Thy *turtle-dove* unto the multitude of
the wicked: for the dark places of the earth are
full of the habitations of cruelty."

Let the man who is in the habit of furnishing
birds for shooting matches read and ponder over
this passage of Scripture, and let those who deny

that animals have souls erase that word from God's Revelation or admit they are wrong

In reading the history of the world it is interesting to note the evolution in morality. What was once thought moral is now known to be immoral, and what was once thought innocent is now known to be wicked.

The teachings of the most cultured people of ancient times, the Greeks and Romans, would to-day be considered barbarous, tyrannical, and cruel In their form of government the condition of slaves and women were on an equality, and man and lower animals were tortured with the most horrible cruelties for the amusement of the people.

Man was compelled to fight against man, and the ladies of the empire, the female aristocracy, gazed upon man plunging the sword in the breast of man and the bloody and agonizing struggle of death with triumphant joy.

Starved lions, dogs, and bears were placed in the arena of the theatre with sheep, goats, and cattle, and the bloody struggle for life was witnessed by men, women, and children of the nation.

But retribution will come upon nations as well as individuals for wrong-doing. Look at the history of the Antediluvians, Sodom and Gomorrah, Egypt, Canaan, Nineveh, Babylon and Persia. And later on, consider the history of the once proud and prosperous nations of Greece and Rome, which were permitted to continue for a thousand years and then were blotted from the face of the earth.

The cry of the oppressed may be unheeded on earth but it is heard in heaven God is just; and if justice reigns, then the unjust must sooner or later suffer terrible retribution, for " Vengeance is Mine ; I will repay saith the Lord."

Sporting at the sacrifice of suffering is a relic of barbarism, and how any refined sensitive human being can engage in such amusement is more than I can comprehend. What may be called sport, to one of God's creatures becomes intense suffering and death

The wholesale slaughter of birds to furnish ornaments for women's hats is another feature of wanton cruelty which deserves the condemnation of all good people.

When a woman is wearing the form of a beautiful bird, with bright and lovely plumage, its feet clinging as it were to the limb of a tree, its wings spread as if about to soar to the heavens, and its tiny mouth partly open as if its song had been cut short by the assassin's bullet, does she realize that that dead form was once a precious creature, happy in its forest home, with a warm heart and a living soul? And yet this is true if the Bible is true.

The remedy is obvious. Do not wear such ornaments, and by so doing, stop the demand.

We should blush with shame and tremble with remorse to be the cause of the death of the sweet birds which enliven our homes by their happy lives. Their sweet songs awake us at the dawn, accompany us through the day, and at soft twilight their plaintive lullabies of praise and thankfulness to God who created them for our happiness, soften and harmonize our best natures.

The beneficent Creator seems to spare no pains in providing such means to cheer the hearts of mankind, and to lessen his sorrows. How sweetly at the return of spring, do the notes of the brown thrush, the robin and the meadow-lark burst upon our ears, as a reminder of our childhood days. No inducement should cause us to cut short the precious life of one of these little creatures.

While with many of us the haunts of the green meadows and the maple forests, like a dream, have faded away through the lapse of time, yet we have our homes, our lawns and parks, and can care for and love the birds the more for past associations.

Seal hunting is another cruelty which should not be overlooked or passed uncensured. These harmless animals are slaughtered in March when the baby seals are too young and helpless to get out of the way of the hunters, and when they are dependent upon their mother's milk for support.

While a large number of the young seals are killed in the absence of their mothers, yet thousands of mother seals are slaughtered annually in the absence of their young which are left to suffer and starve to death. Statistics show that there have been about two hundred thousand killed annually, and it is feared by those who profit by this slaughter, that the species will soon become exterminated. When contemplating this cruel wholesale slaughter, and the fact that our government encourages it, and receives a large sum of blood-money annually for this gracious privilege, I can only wish that God in His infinite love and mercy, might see fit to call to Himself the soul of the last one. Extermination has been the fate of some of the most noble animals which formerly roamed

over the hills and western prairies of our land,
and of some species of birds of most beautiful
plumage, which enlivened the forests with their
sweetest songs "The Lord is very pitiful and of
tender mercy," and when any species of His creatures are so tortured that all life becomes an endless misery He calls them to Himself.

Fashion, like sporting, is planted deep in human nature, and is often productive of great evil.
Fashion is responsible for the way horses are
abused by curb-bits, double bits, over-head check-
reins, and docking Any one who respects the
moral law will agree that a horse has a right to be
protected from cruel torment. The over-check does
not have a single argument in its favor. It makes
a horse carry his head in an unnatural position
which is neither graceful, comfortable, nor benefi-
cial. He is more apt to stumble, as he cannot see
his feet, and when required to draw a heavy load
the check holds up his head and shoulders, the very
reverse of a natural position for a heavy draught.
It interferes with the graceful appearance of a
horse, and detracts from his natural, easy movements It obstructs breathing, and on a long journey causes intense suffering by holding the head in

one position. That it causes a horse to suffer is evident by the way he frets, tossing his head from side to side, foaming and often bleeding from the constant pressure on the tender parts of the mouth and tongue It makes the mouth raw and sore, creates distress, and consequently the horse becomes irritable and less kind and useful, and his life is shortened The best argument is the comparison of livery horses with farm horses of the same age.

When two bits are used in the mouth, the objections to the over-check are still greater. The mouth is distorted and spread apart; dust accumulates in the mouth and throat, and breathing is seriously interfered with. Curb-bits are equally objectionable They are a constant misery in a horse's mouth as they press up on the chin and down on the tongue and tender parts of the mouth. The long levers are not in the proper position to guide or control a horse and such a bit should never be used under any circumstances.

A horse is a kind, gentle, obedient animal, and is willing to do what he understands is required of him, but, like a child, he must be taught. There are three important things in the government and control of all animals, namely, common sense, patience, and kindness, each of which is indispensable.

The fashion of docking horses is prohibited in several states, and should be in all. It is an agonizing, useless operation, and inflicts on the poor horse a cruel mutilation for life. When a portion of the tail is amputated it destroys the graceful movements and noble appearance the Creator has given to a perfect horse, to say nothing of his inability to dislodge flies and dust from his body. The "Rural Stockman," of New Orleans, declares: "When men commit such a cruelty as docking horses they give good evidence that the whipping-post was abolished too soon." Dr. George Fleming, late Chief Veterinary Surgeon of England, says, "Nothing can be more disgusting than this barbarous and detestable fashion. Those who sanction it are no true horsemen, but are promoters of a great cruelty which decreases the usefulness and value of horses." Dr. S. K. Johnson, Chief Surgeon New York Veterinary Hospital, gives his opinion in the following words: "No language can be too strong in condemnation of the painful and cruel operation called docking." We are glad to know that this sinful habit is on the decrease.

On the Western plains, horses, sheep, and cattle are raised in large numbers, and the suffering they endure, during winters, especially, is horrible. As a rule, the large herds are not protected from the snow-storms, and thousands starve and freeze to death every year. While young, they are branded with red-hot irons, and many of them are rebranded many times When they are finally shipped, they undergo great suffering from being overcrowded and exposed to heat and cold, and, in addition, are often starved and beaten and mutilated by the drovers. Like human slavery of old, the suffering of living beings is not taken into consideration when there is prospect of financial gain.

CHAPTER XVII

SOME PROMINENT EVILS —A NECESSITY FOR A FUTURE REWARD

Duty of Christian people—No excuse for wanton cruelty—Laws should be made and enforced against it—Animals have rights—God will finally redeem all His creatures.

THE most lamentable trait in human nature is man's willingness to sacrifice the sense of right upon the altar of cruelty in order to advance his personal interest. The fad to be called "scientific," at the expense of cruelty, has become fashionable in the last century. It is the revival of the worst forms of heathen barbarism, and is endangering the good name, peace, and happiness of our country.

The moral law of justice, of love, and of mercy is being supplanted by injustice and cruelty. Man becomes so hardened by selfishness that if the life of a lower animal or a human being stands in his supposed way to notoriety he regards them as mere things to be destroyed. This growing propensity should arouse all good, law-abiding people to make a united effort to prohibit all forms of wanton cruelty It seems a great misfortune that in this age of reform, when the Christian world is becoming hopeful, and mankind as a general rule, growing better, that a few inhumane physiologists should insist on shocking, not only the Christian world, but the heathen world, by using the most sickening tortures the devilish nature of man can invent on the living bodies of sensitive beings Good people are powerless to help, but they turn aside and weep at the indescribable miseries and horrors inflicted upon animals.

Vivisection has been brought to public notice in the last few years by the continued and persistent barbarous experiments, under the guise of physiological science, made on our most gentle and loving animals by the hands of cruel men. Like many other evils which have blotted the pages of the history of man with crime and blood, this is destined to continue until the people rise in a mass and cry out, it is enough. How long these poor defenseless animals will be permitted to suffer before that time comes is a heart-breaking problem for kind and good men and women to solve.

We are constantly talking and writing about the

cruelties of other nations while we are permitting
worse things frequently in our own country.

There is a tendency among even Christian people
to overlook the subject of cruelty to animals, and
regard it as only a mere fancy of sentimentalism.
We do not hope to reform that class so much as
to educate the rising generation to a higher and
nobler sentiment. It is the young mind, now in a
process of cultivation and discipline, that we expect
to influence for good. When we look over the pages
of history and see the vast amount of time, money,
and suffering it takes to bring about any great
reform, our hearts are made to ache at the sinful
nature of man. The efforts which are being made
to-day by many of the best people in the civilized
world to prohibit vivisection should have the support of all Christian people of all nations, and I
believe the cause does have their support. Right
here is where the line should be drawn ; if a man
or woman refuses to help support this great humane
cause, he or she cannot possibly be a Christian according to the teachings of the Bible, which says,
" Open thy mouth for the dumb . . . be merciful
as your Father is merciful . . . what doth the
Lord require of thee but to do justly, love mercy,

and walk humbly with thy God . . . a righteous man regardeth the life of his beast, but the tender mercies of the wicked are cruel . . . blessed are the merciful . . . be ye kind and tender-hearted . . . be ye harmless as doves . . the righteous is ever merciful . . . he shall be judged without mercy who shows no mercy."

People are generally uninformed on this subject. I have had a number of ministers frankly acknowledge they did not know the true import of the word *vivisection*, and were not aware of the extent of its practice It may be said that such things are too horrible to read, but it must be remembered that they are not too horrible to be done by murderous hands, and not so horrible but that the poor animals are compelled to endure the suffering.

Reforms are brought about by holding up the oppressors to the gaze of the world in their true light. The oppression and cruelty practiced by the Inquisition and slavery were suppressed when the masses became enlightened on the subject, and united in concerted action to blot them out of existence. God will hear the cry of the oppressed. It was not His will but man's disobedience which brought sin and suffering into the world. To suppose that God, in the creation of animals, gave them a system of sensory nerves to be used for experimental purposes by man would be the greatest blasphemy which could possibly be attributed to a beneficent Creator.

God never made it necessary to vivisect His innocent, helpless creatures in order to find the secrets of the science of biology, physiology, or anatomy Shame on any mortal man who would dare claim that such a horrible and repulsive method of investigation became necessary. As the science of anatomy and physiology is reduced to a perfect and complete system, it becomes entirely unnecessary to resort to the cruel and sickening methods practiced by some anatomists and physiologists.

The quickest and best way to study anatomy and physiology is by the use of books, charts, maps, models, skeletons, manikins, and various illustrations, all to be had at a small cost. All well-regulated schools and colleges are supplied with the means necessary to teach all that can be learned, and the practice of vivisection cannot possibly add anything new or useful. If a student wishes to study for the practice of medicine and surgery, then it may become necessary to take a practical course in the dissecting-room, but in no case is vivisection of any practical value whatever.

I hold a diploma from one of the largest and best-equipped medical colleges in the United States, and I have never known nor heard of a single case of vivisection ever having been practiced within its grand old walls.

The practice of vivisection is not done for the good of humanity, but simply to keep up with a useless fad which has been recently introduced into the curriculum of college laboratory work. The desire to have the most extensive course has been at the bottom of it all, and yet there are very few of our most talented and useful teachers and physicians who approve of such a course

With all our national sins, so many and so varied, the neglect to protect animals against suffering and wanton cruelty is the worst and the least excusable.

We look to moral influences and an enlightened education to overcome prejudices and prevailing errors. By far the greater number of opinions on which we act in life are adopted upon the authority of others, and in this way a system of education

may be formed which is opposed to moral truth.
Education is valuable only in proportion as it
makes the world better and happier, and there is
no safe guide for leading the multitude except an
enlightened and moral education. The principal
errors we find may be attributed to motives
springing from the pride and the perverse disposition of the human heart, prompted by a mere intellectual enthusiasm. Errors generated in this
manner possess, commonly, some aspect of beauty,
of greatness, or of philosophical simplicity, to
recommend them; for as they were framed amid a
pleasurable excitement of the mind, so they will
have a power to convey a kindred delight to
others But the mischief is often more active and
conspicuous in second hands than in those of its
author. Imitators become more indiscreet and
radical than the originators

But whoever in any manner cuts himself off
from the common sympathies of our best nature
by making sport of the energies of moral action,
rebutting every idea that does not minister gratification either to fancy or taste, and having recourse
either to a jargon of sophistries, or to trivial eva-
sions, when other men act upon the intuitions of

good sense and right motives,—such a man becomes dangerous to the welfare of any community. Moral restraint serves directly to dispel errors of opinion by presenting the sense of justice and mercy as a true guide.

Christianity, unlike human science, was given to mankind in a finished form, and cannot be improved but simply learned by the guidance of an enlightened conscience. Love and mercy form the principal attributes of all virtue, hence we should

> "Pity the sorrows of a poor old dog,
>   Who wags his tail a-begging in his need ;
> Despise not even the sorrows of a frog,
>   God's creatures too, and that's enough to plead ;
> Spare puss, who trusts us, purring on our hearth ;
>   Spare bunny, once so frisky and so free ,
> Spare all the harmless tenants of the earth ;
>   Spare and be spared—or who shall plead for thee?"

The divine law and teachings are a sure and safe standard of right and duty, and form a proper rule of human ethics. This enthroned in the heart and life will secure the happiness of the individual, and best promote the highest good of society and the happiness of the world.

The efforts of man to utilize a thing for his selfish purpose regardless of the moral law governing such utility has formed the dark side of the human race during all ages. To use a thing, without regard to the proper use the moral law intended, is subverting its purpose and degrading the omniscient power and goodness of the Creator Right, wrongly interpreted as to what might appear to be useful, has been the palliating excuse for the most abominable cruelties and wrongs ever practiced by man. Good people who conscientiously differ from others were once regarded as heretics, and injurious to the highest welfare of the country ; and, under the idea of utility, were put to death by the thousands

Not many centuries ago slaves were bought for the purpose of experimenting on by vivisection, and as it was supposed to be for the utility of science, the right to do so was granted. Now since slaves are not in the market, poor, helpless, innocent animals are made the prey for the supposed utility of scientific investigation with all the recurrent horrors of the dark ages.

Man has no more moral right to the one than to the other, as both are a usurpation of a power of the strong over the weak, for selfish and wicked purposes.

H. S. Salt, in Animals' Rights, makes this bold

assertion: "The present condition of the more highly organized domestic animals is in many ways very analogous to that of the slaves of a hundred years ago. Look back, and you will find in their case precisely the same exclusion; and, as a consequence, the same deliberate stubborn denial of their social rights. Look back, for it is well to do so; and then look forward, and the moral can hardly be mistaken."

The whole structure of society is based on the fact of human responsibility. If men are not accountable for their actions, then there can be no justice, no law, no assurance of the rights of the oppressed and suffering. Hence the necessity for laws to punish those who cannot be persuaded by gentle means. Without the prevalence of laws to restrain the vicious, civil government could not exist.

Some persons may try to evade the moral responsibility portrayed in this unpretending volume; but a guilty conscience will not allow them to do so. No person can see intense suffering with the power to relieve it, and not do so, unless his conscience is seared with the blackest of crimes and the most dissolute cruelties.

In conclusion, and with direct reference to the

theme of this book, let me urge that one of the principal arguments for man's immortality is that righteousness is not always rewarded in this world, and sin is not always punished. The sinner may be prosperous and happy, so far as this world is concerned, and the righteous may be subjected to perpetual want and misery The innocent may be cruelly tortured to death, like the Christian martyrs and lower animals, and the wicked devils who perpetrate such deeds enjoy the happiness and luxury of a palatial home.

It is claimed that there must be a future life in order to equalize such differences, which seems reasonable. If such is God's plan to adjust the differences in one species of His creatures, by what justice could He exclude another species who are possessed of a like nervous system and susceptible of like mental sorrow and physical suffering?

Is it in accordance with the laws of nature and what we know of the All-wise Creator to make such a break in a general law as to give man a reward of eternal happiness for innocence and suffering, and annihilate another species of His creatures for the same reason?

That all living beings are immortal, and will con-

tinue to live in another world, is the only possible
way finite minds can solve the question as to why
the innocent and good are often compelled to endure greater suffering than the wicked. The differences of features, races, species, powers of intellect,
whether the creatures walk, hop, swim or fly,
whether they go on two or four legs, will never
solve the question, for God made every bone, muscle,
and sinew, and strung each body with a system of
sensor nerves, and gave to each its own identity and
individuality, without consulting the wish or
choice of the creature. If there is a God who rules
the universe and impartially deals out justice and
mercy, who has given to man and lower animals
the five senses, and made them capable of pleasure
and pain, and permits such evident inequality on
earth, is it not reasonable to believe He will correct
this sad defect in a better world to come, where

> " We may enjoy in realms above
> The blessings of eternal love :
> When man, released from pain and care,
> With bird and beast shall heaven share ? "
>
> —MOOR.

THE END

CPSIA information can be obtained at www.ICGtesting.com
Printed in the USA
LVOW03s1637290514

387768LV00017B/69/P

9 781293 799765